LOOK DOWN THAT WINDING RIVER

BOOKS BY BEN LUCIEN BURMAN

Blow a Wild Bugle for Catfish Bend
The Owl Hoots Twice at Catfish Bend
Seven Stars for Catfish Bend
High Water at Catfish Bend
Three from Catfish Bend *
The Sign of the Praying Tiger
The Street of the Laughing Camel
The Four Lives of Mundy Tolliver
Everywhere I Roam
Rooster Crows for a Day
Blow for a Landing
Steamboat Round the Bend
Mississippi
The Generals Wear Cork Hats
It's a Big Continent
It's a Big Country
Children of Noah
Miracle on the Congo
Big River to Cross

* *Omnibus volume containing the three titles immediately preceding.*

with a foreword by JOHN K. HUTCHENS

illustrations by ALICE CADDY

Taplinger Publishing Company · New York

LOOK DOWN THAT WINDING RIVER

an informal profile of the MISSISSIPPI

BEN LUCIEN BURMAN

First Edition
Published in the United States in 1973 by
TAPLINGER PUBLISHING CO., INC.
New York, New York

Chapter 10, "A Voyage of Roses," first appeared in the Reader's Digest, March 1973.

Published simultaneously in the Dominion of Canada by Burns & MacEachern, Ltd., Toronto

Library of Congress Catalog Card Number: 72-6610

ISBN 0-8008-4960-4

Designed by The Etheredges

FOR HOBE LEWIS AND BUN MAHONY
GENEROUS AND UNCOMPLAINING GODFATHERS
OF THE ERRANT AUTHOR
AS HE WANDERED THE RIVER
AND THE FAR PLACES OF THE EARTH

A TIMELY NOTE

The author's experiences recorded in the chapters involving the *Tennessee Belle* took place chiefly in the Twenties and Thirties, in the period between the First and Second World Wars. The happenings on the other boats mentioned occurred mostly in the Thirties and Forties, with the exception of the final chapter, where the time is the present.

. . . . .

ACKNOWLEDGMENTS

I am happy to acknowledge my deep-felt debt of gratitude to the magazines in which so many of my pieces on the River have appeared over the years and from which I have drawn occasional ancedotes and other material for some of the chapters in the present volume: to the *Reader's Digest* in particular for innumerable articles, notably "Steamboat on the River," "The Golden Age of the Steamboats," "At Home in the Hills," "Last Pioneers," "Living as They Please," and a condensed version of "The Mississippi Revisited"; to *Harper's Magazine* for "Mississippi Roustabouts"; to the *Saturday Evening Post* for "Shantyboat"; to *Collier's* for "The Chinese Shrimp Platforms," and to the *Saturday Review* for "Music on the Mississippi."

CONTENTS

9

CONTENTS

FOREWORD

Where Licking River flows into a somewhat larger one, the Ohio, there is Covington, Kentucky, and there was a boy named Ben Lucien Burman who even then, some seventy years ago, knew he was going to be a writer. Before he would get around to doing much about this, he would go away from Covington for his formal education, fight in a war in Europe, and work on newspapers in Boston and New York. But down deep he must have known what mattered most to him and was waiting for him back home: the mighty river to which the little Licking and the big Ohio, along with a number of others, contribute not only water but lore and legend, people and boats. He would come to know them all, whether to report about them as a traveler or shape them in fancy as an artist, and on one memorable occasion to create a world within that world: in the enchanting wonderland known as Catfish Bend, where his friends the raccoon, the fox, and the bullfrog hold forth so happily.

Looking back, after all he has written so truly and eloquently about the river, it is notable that even one of his earliest, very young river stories contains an enduring Burman theme; he has a character say, "River is a beautiful thing. More than that she's a holy thing. Don't need to go to church when you're on the river."

Beautiful, yes, but with terrors to match its glories. For as the pages that follow this introductory note attest, Ben Burman— romantic though he is—does not sentimentalize. If he recalls tenderly the rough, dangerous, highly individualistic river life of the past, it is to contrast it with the computerized present. A complexly mechanized modern towboat has its agreeable creature comforts, but who would trade a day on one for ten minutes with the "sweet-sounding whistles and the splashing paddlewheels" of the great river steamers of other days?

Mr. Burman wouldn't, I suspect, nor would we who have traveled with him up and down the river through the years in such fiction as *Steamboat Round the Bend* and *Blow for a Landing,* and listened as he told stories, in that wonderfully easy, conversational style of his, in *Big River to Cross.* A Burman devotee is one who feels himself a friend of the old Beaver Slough doctor-turned-steamboater, Captain John, steering his *Bayou Queen* proudly through *Steamboat Round the Bend,* and Willow Joe, the dreamy musician, who walks on water in *Blow for a Landing.* As for Mr. Burman's Catfish Bend, there are said to be dwellers in the vicinity of Vicksburg who swear that tourists have asked in all seriousness how to get to that kingdom of Judge Black, the kindly blacksnake, and J. C. Hunter, the flashy red fox, and wise old Doc Raccoon. Nor is this so odd as it may seem, for they too live in the mind of an imaginative reader as vividly as those back-country moonshiners whose sturdy independence fills our guide with admiration.

Now we are with him once more on another sort of river trip, a quite personal one, consisting in large part of memories of the river as it was, with a concluding and not altogether disapproving view of the river as it is today. Almost at once we meet folks who almost certainly were the prototypes of characters in the novels, like Captain Dick Dicharry of the *Tennessee Belle,* who actually entrusted his beautiful craft in the dark of the night to the cub-pilot Burman, and the wild shantyboaters who feuded endlessly with the pilots who steamed close to shore and rocked the flimsy shanties for sport, and Captain Bill Menke of the showboat *Goldenrod,* whose noble calliope obligingly played "Nearer, My God, to Thee" at the request of a prisoner awaiting execution in Louisiana.

No chronicler of the river since Mark Twain has given us so warm and intimate a portrait, so bountiful in tall tales and true ones (but the tall ones have their own truth), the speech of pilots, engineers and roustabouts, the sound of a boat's bell the sweeter for silver dollars tossed into the molten iron when it was being cast. Were there cranes that guided a boat through heavy fog, and a porpoise that picked up corpses floating in the Gulf and brought them ashore for Christian burial, cats that predicted hurricanes with absolute accuracy? If Ben Burman says so, I believe it. At any rate, I believe that he heard anything he says he heard, and surely he is one of the superb listeners among writing men of his time. You can all but see him cocking an ear when he hears an old-timer say, "Steamboat coffee ain't no good unless when you put a spoon in it she stands up," or when he drops off to sleep on the *Tennessee Belle* hearing a roustabout sing:

> *Roustabout ain't got no home,*
> *Makes his living from his shoulder bone.*
> *Break a line, borrow another.*
> *Black man die, hire his brother.*

And now? Now, on 5000-horsepower towboat pushing a quarter of a mile of barges through a storm that would have been too much for the old *Tennessee Belle,* young deckhands eat gourmet food, sleep in air-conditioned quarters, and call the captain by his first name. But, as you are about to see, it's still Ben Lucien

Burman's river. It always will be, and thanks to him it can be yours, too, even if you never get close enough to it to see the river light the United States Coast Guard has named for him near Baton Rouge. (Who needs a Nobel Prize after that?)

All this is by way of saying he has created that rarity in modern American literature: a body of work that gives every promise of becoming a permanent fixture in our culture. Its music is haunting. Its realism is a form of social history. Its narrative power is in the timeless tradition of all great storytelling.

So the mighty river flows, the working boats push their way upstream and glide south to the Gulf, and Ben Lucien Burman writes on. The more things change . . .

JOHN K. HUTCHENS

A
GLANCE BACKWARD

I am a very lucky man. I was born beside water. Mountain peaks are beautiful and deserts are inspiring. But they cannot compare with the tranquil joy of sitting beside the sea or a river. After all, unless the scientists are wrong, we rose out of the water. Our present life on the land is only an afterthought.

I fell in love with the river as a child of perhaps three or four when I took my first steamboat trip on the Ohio. I can still hear that hushed coughing of the smokestacks, unlike any other sound in the world, as the boat moved between the low hills up the yellow water; I can still remember my childish awe as at night I watched the rays of the gigantic searchlight sweeping the willowed shore for a landing.

The first river people that I knew were those I met as I was growing up in up hometown of Covington in Kentucky, probably not a very exciting place in those days for the casual tourist to visit, unless he was a racehorse devotee ready to lose all his money at the track in Latonia. But under the quiet surface lay riches that to me were fit for the treasury of a king. The town lay at the junction of the Ohio and Licking rivers. On the Ohio often I saw the steamboats passing on their way from Pittsburgh to New Orleans with their tows of coal and steel; every day in the hot summers I heard the calliope of the *Island Queen* sending out its steamy melodies to lure any perspiring travelers within hearing to come and enjoy the cooling breezes born on the river. On the Licking, summer or winter, I could call on the shantyboatmen who lived in their battered dwellings on the bank, and listen to their rich philosophy.

There was a whole settlement along the Licking of shanty-boaters and other rebels against conventional society, so wild it was known as Oklahoma; and though it was strictly off limits for small boys I somehow managed occasionally to chat with some of the inhabitants. In the town marketplace every Saturday there would be a blind ballad singer drifted down from the Hatfield-McCoy country in the hills a little more than a hundred miles away; in the churches of the black people I heard their rich voices, raised in fervent praise of Jesus and the Lord who had given them so little.

I am a very lucky man.

I always wanted to be a writer. Publishers' publicity releases have often said that I wrote my first story at the age of seven on a toy typewriter; unlike the statements at times in publicity releases this one happens to be true. In those days wanting to be a writer was something akin to lunacy; all writers were either lethal drunk-ards like Edgar Allan Poe or unfortunate drug addicts like Samuel Coleridge. But my surroundings and my desires were stronger than any such hindrances. I went off to college, and returning home with ink still in my blood, renewed my love for the river. But the river there had changed greatly; the Ohio was becoming industrial-ized.

I moved farther south to Memphis and New Orleans, where the river life had been far less affected. I met Captain Dick Dicharry of the *Tennessee Belle;* regal gambler that he was, he took a frightful chance and made me a cub pilot on his boat so that what I wrote would not seem too foolish in the eyes of rivermen. I remember the night when I was standing the graveyard watch in the pilot house at three o'clock in the morning and my cherished, long-suffering wife came up and found I was at the wheel alone in the middle of the black Mississippi. Her confidence didn't equal that of Captain Dick. She hasn't recovered from the shock even now.

On other steamboats I traveled the river from its placid beginnings in the North to where the porpoise play in its spreading waters as it flows into the blue Gulf; I traveled the tributaries until they became turbulent mountain streams, haunted by sun-bonneted women and rifle-carrying moonshiners; I steamed past the white-pillared mansions on the great plantations of the South and the pitiful cabins of the sharecroppers; I listened to the chanting of the roustabouts and the clanking of shovels heaping coal into the glowing fireboxes, while the churning paddlewheels played a muted accompaniment.

Then suddenly overnight the steamboats were gone, mortally wounded first by the railroads, then by the trucks and the snorting automobiles and by a world which had no time for leisure. The old wood-burning *Ouchita,* like a feeble old man abandoned by his family, died a pathetic death in the steamboat boneyard. The *Tennessee Belle* went up in a blaze of glory and lies a charred hulk at the bottom of the Mississippi.

But I knew and loved them and their royal sisters before they died, in their happy days when they were the queens of the river.

Now there are new, different queens on the Mississippi, magnificent towboats of enormous power, equipped with every comfort of sophisticated living and manned by young, unsophisticated rivermen from the sleepy towns and villages along the shore. Lately I have known this new life also. I have seen how when the new paint on the towboats has flaked in faint patches and the young men have mellowed a little with age and watery wisdom, the river once more acquires its earlier charm and fascination. It is the old river, in a new reincarnation.

I am a very lucky man.

BEN LUCIEN BURMAN

PART

1

THE WAY
IT
USED TO BE

CHAPTER

1

PADDLEWHEELS
AND
PILOTS

The first sound I can remember is the whistle of a steamboat. I heard it many times afterward in my childhood. To my ears the melancholy tones were wonderful music, a glorious symphony performed by the world's greatest orchestra. I little realized it was soon to be a requiem played for perhaps the most colorful epoch of all our fantastic history, the era of the Mississippi steamboat.

It was anything but an era of perfection. It was bawdy, it was violent, it was often cruel. But in vivid contrast to our cold mechanical age where every village and town is the exact copy of every other and computers have taken the place of our souls, it was a life full of beauty and humor and rich humanity.

I shall never forget the starlit night as I sat in the pilot house of the steamboat *Tennessee Belle*, listening for the first time to the black giant at the bow taking soundings that would guide the

steersman through a difficult stretch of the ever-changing river. Mournfully his chanting drifted across the dark water: "No-o-o-o Bottom! There is No-o-o-o Bottom!" A moment later a dwarfish black man on the texas deck below me echoed the cry: "No-o-o-o Bottom! There is No-o-o-o Bottom!" in a poignant melody that seemed to reflect all the tragedy from the days his ancestors were brought in chains on slave ships from the fever-laden Congo. I remember how the voice of Captain Dick Dicharry, the boat's owner, boomed out an indignant command and the noisy voices of the crew below, engaged in some argument, grew hushed until the chant, like a sacred ritual, was ended.

"Got the best singers on the river," Captain Dick told me. "Don't care if a leadsman's the best in the world. Won't have him unless he can sing. Rather wreck my boat."

An automobile is the giddy creature of a nerve-racked world, fit only to speed its owner off to a sanitarium where he may recover from the frenzy it helped to induce. An automobile will jolt the

the traveler from New Orleans to Greenville, Mississippi, in less than eight hours. On a steamboat the round trip required two weeks. For the steamboat was of a courtly, gentle breed, who knew that not in fever but in leisure and grace lay the secret of a happy life. When a packetboat saw an old Negro waving a battered hat on the shore, she stopped to take him aboard with his woebegone dog and his fragment of a stove; if she saw a fire burning at night along the edge of a piny wood, she steamed carefully toward it and waited patiently till the grizzled farmer standing there had driven his squealing pigs up the muddy gangplank.

The captains of the steamboats formed a unique company. There were famous figures in the old days, like the captains of the *Natchez* and the *Robert E. Lee*. There were men in my own day like Captain Dick, known as the last King of the Lower Mississippi. Born a poor boy, unlike many captains, his first boat was the *Uncle Oliver* which he had managed to buy with great difficulty, a paintless relic with a limping smokestack, so covered with soot the black roustabouts renamed her the *Dirty Face*. Times were hard and cargoes elusive as the foxes off in the distant hills. Captain Dick, in New Orleans, lacked even the money to buy enough coal to take the *Dirty Face* all the way to Greenville, the usual end of her run. The boat started on the trip, nevertheless, and was in the middle of the river, miles from anywhere, when the mate came running to the pilot house to tell Captain Dick the last lump in the coal bins was finished; in a few minutes the boat would start drifting helplessly down the water.

"Tear up the deck floor!" shouted Captain Dick.

An instant later there was a noise below of wrenching crowbars and crashing axes as the floorboards were ripped free and tossed into fireboxes. The *Dirty Face* steamed merrily on to Natchez, where on the wharf a heaven-sent mountain of cotton bales was waiting.

The crews of the boats were characters, like their commanders. There was Barney, the engineer of the *Tennessee Belle,* who every afternoon would lower a bucket into the murky river, and when it was full of the muddy liquid "too thick to navigate, too thin to cultivate," would gulp down a brown quart or two. "Keeps my health a-going good," he would tell me. "That's the trouble with people nowadays. That's what's causing all this sickness. It's this filtering the water. Takes all the strength out of it."

There was the engineer called Blue Johnny, noted for his tippling, who each morning would go up to the pilot house and say to the steersman, "Captain, give me the orders for everything you want me to do the rest of the day, 'cause in an hour I'm going to be drunk and then I won't be able to understand 'em."

There was Captain Sam, the mate, whose favorite food was hard-boiled eggs. But his way of eating them was singular. He sprinkled salt and pepper on the shell and swallowed the egg whole. There was the Cajun pilot I knew who hated alligators. Whenever he saw an alligator in a bayou where the boat was traveling he would give the steering wheel to his partner, and leaping over the side, would wrestle with the monstrous reptile until it was exhausted and he could haul it triumphantly aboard.

The boats themselves were characters, acquiring peculiarities that, like the *Dirty Face,* gave them nicknames from which they never escaped. The *Sprague,* largest towboat ever to run the river, and capable of hauling an incredible number of barges loaded with incredible tons of freight, was known affectionately as *Big Mama;* the *Kurzweg,* because she was powered by a Diesel engine and thus lacked the asthmatic cough of her steamy sisters, was contemptuously known as the *Deaf and Dumb Boat.*

The *Vernie Swain* was famous for its wildcat whistle, an eerie cry calculated to make the bravest lion flee in panic. The first night the boat steamed down the river the delighted pilot rarely took his hand off the whistle cord. In the morning, legend says, the farmers on both banks took their rifles and organized posses to hunt the sudden terror.

"Worst panther ever in the country," said an Arkansas cracker as he loaded his gun at the crossroads store where he had bought a supply of ammunition. "I heard it hollering all night."

The lanky farmer beside him nodded in agreement. "It's wild

and hungry," he said. "And it's moving fast. I know, 'cause I seen its tracks."

Another boat, rumor declared, was so leaky and full of water the captain kept a skiff down in her hold so the carpenter could row back and forth and patch the breaks more conveniently.

Among the most colorful vessels on which I traveled was the last woodburner, the venerable *Ouchita*. Everywhere on the banks as she steamed along were mounds of sawed pine waiting to feed her hungry boilers. The wood was a favorite hiding place for snakes; every now and then as we landed I would hear a shout and peals of laughter from the roustabouts as one of their number bringing the timber aboard discovered he was also carrying a giant rattler. The boat's progress was a continuous shower of sparks and red-hot embers spouting from her smokestacks like giant Fourth of July flowerpots, and wreaking havoc on the clothing of any traveler who chanced to be below. I can still see the desperate faces and still hear the agonized cries of the watchmen at the huge Standard Oil refinery at Baton Rouge as we chugged past, spouting our private volcanic eruption.

Why we failed to send the entire refinery up in flames is a riddle that only Old Al, the great alligator who presides over the Mississippi, can possibly explain.

Most captains were genial men who cherished their boats as a doting father cherishes his favorite child. No matter how important a business discussion might be, no matter how intense the conversation, Captain Dick would always interrupt whenever the whistle of the *Tennessee Belle* started to blow; he would listen raptly as though he were hearing the celestial music of the spheres.

If anyone protested Captain Dick would wither him with some sharp Cajun sarcasm and add tartly, "Ain't any talk in the world worth the whistle of the *Belle*."

But occasionally there was a misanthrope, lacking such sentiment and affection. Captain Dick was talking one day with a captain whose boat in a nearby trade had been damaged beyond repair and was on its way to the steamboat graveyard.

Captain Dick expressed his sympathy.

To his amazement the other riverman, noted for his insensitive nature, only shrugged his shoulders. "What's a steamboat?" he demanded. "Just some deckboards, a paddlewheel, and a fool in a pilot house."

Captain Dick grew hot with anger. "Thought you were my friend," he retorted. "Now I know better. You don't feel bad when your steamboat dies; I know you won't waste half a minute worrying when I die. You're too cold a man for me. We're through."

This callous individual was blood brother to the perhaps mythical Captain Jeff whose acquaintance I made one night in the pilot house of the *Belle*. To my surprise I saw the pilot suddenly reach for the whistle cord and blow a long blast that echoed dolefully over the water. I could see nothing ahead and asked the reason.

"I'm blowing for Captain Jeff," the pilot answered. "He's buried on top of that bluff over yonder. Jeff was an old steamboat captain with a terrible temper. Toward the end he got tired of all the troubles he was having with other pilots harassing him; before he died he asked his family to build a tomb on the bluff with a little window on the river side and stand his coffin on end so he could look out and curse all the steamboat captains passing. Roustabouts say if you don't whistle when you pass he'll sink you before the next trip."

The whistle was always of great significance to a roustabout. Often a pilot was judged not by his expertness as a pilot but by the length of time he blew a whistle. A short-whistling pilot was a certain carrier of bad luck; roustabouts, when they could, avoided his company as if he were a sort of steamboat Typhoid Mary.

A long blast of the whistle was sometimes useful for diplomatic reasons as well.

"A captain that don't blow a long whistle can git you into mighty bad trouble," said Mouse, a beady-eyed little roustabout on the *Ouchita*. "If your boat's laid up and you're calling on a lady that's the girl friend of a roustabout on some other boat, when the pilot of that boat blows a long whistle that he's coming home you got plenty of time to get away. But if he's one of them short-blowing fellows in a minute the rouster's at the front door and you got to run for your life."

Even to those much higher in the social scale than a roustabout the whistle had great importance. The owners of the plantations along the banks became attached to a certain whistle and gave the boat bearing it their profitable commerce. When Captain Dick was waging a David-and-Goliath battle with the Illinois Cen-

tral for the cotton trade, the railroad somehow obtained the exact measurements of the *Tennessee Belle*'s beautiful whistle and attempted to duplicate the tone on the company's locomotives. To Captain Dick's joy the attempt was a disaster.

A long time ago, to learn the river so that what I wrote would be the truth, I shipped as a sometime cub pilot on the *Tennessee Belle*. My first trip on the river at night was a voyage into the incredible. It seemed little short of the miraculous when the senior pilot, the quiet, philosophic Captain Charley Barker, casually glanced down the water where I could see only abysmal blackness, then spun the wheel and landed the boat at a shadowy gap in the vague line of willows that marked the shore as accurately as though he were driving an automobile into a bright-lit filling station. A moment later a score of mules came stamping aboard, dragging behind them the clanking machinery of a levee construction camp. I marveled then how the shadow of a distant clump of cottonwoods, the dim shape of a far-off oak tree, was to that pilot as brilliant a beacon as the lighthouses that guide great ocean liners to safety along some perilous shore.

And though I was on the river many times afterward, and often in the feeble way of a cub, guided a steamboat on its course, I continued to marvel. For just as in Twain's time the pilot was compelled to know all the stream's fantastic vagaries. Of only one thing could he be sure; the channel would not be the same coming down as when he went up forty-eight hours before. If he did not proceed with exceptional care, the boat would go aground on a new reef suddenly formed along Paddy Hen or strike a new snag at Hard Times Light that would pierce the wooden hull like a child's knife thrust into a Christmas drum. For the river remained and still remains basically as it was in the olden days: beautiful, fascinating, terrible, always unpredictable. Within the brief space of three or four years I have seen a huge sand bar form, several miles long and a mile wide, only to disappear overnight in some sweeping yellow onrush.

"Guess you heard the story about the captain grounded on a sand bar," chuckled Captain Dick. "After he tried everything and couldn't get off he knew he'd be stuck there for months till the high water came in the spring. He was a fellow always liked potatoes, French-fried, home-fried, boiled, anyway you cooked 'em. So he planted a crop of the finest kind he could get hold of. Every day he'd go out on the bar and touch up the ground around 'em with a hoe and give 'em just the right amount of water they needed. He nursed those potatoes the way a mother does her first baby. They grew fine and all the fishermen around said they'd never seen such potatoes. He got so interested in the potatoes he pretty near forgot about his boat. And he was getting all ready to harvest 'em the next day when in the night a big flood came. It floated his boat all right and first thing when the sun was up he went to get his potatoes. But where the potato patch'd been there was ten feet of water. The flood had washed the bar and every potato away."

Piloting was difficult on any occasion. But it was fog that required from the steersman extraordinary, almost superhuman qualities. The good fog pilot was the pilot that tied up his boat, ran the river proverb. But there were many who preferred risk to inaction. I knew steersmen, who legend said, could blow the whistle in a ghostly mist, and by listening to the echo, tell whether they were in front of a cliff, a tree, a sand bar, a house, or even a double house.

29

It was fog that gave rise to so much of the river's folklore.

"Best fog pilot I heard of was Captain Jack," said Captain Dick whenever this favorite subject of steamboatmen was mentioned. "There was a bad stretch of the river full of dangerous rocks where Captain Jack ran his boat and he had to be awful careful steering along it, even when the weather was fine. What made it worse, most of the time there was a fog thick as a bowl of good Cajun gumbo. You couldn't see your own nose in front of you. But Captain Jack managed all right. A farmer there had a dog that was a friend of Captain Jack's and whenever his boat came along in the fog Captain Jack just rang his bell. The dog'd run down to the bank and bark his head off, and Captain Jack'd know where he was to the inch.

"But one night in the worst fog they'd ever had on the river Captain Jack rang the bell and didn't get any answer. He rang it again and still he didn't hear anything. So he figured he wasn't near the bad place after all and signaled the engineer to get moving fast. Because of the fog they were two hours behind time. A minute later the boat was breaking up on the rocks. The dog had died the night before."

I heard how Captain Jack, trapped one night in another dense fog, ordered his mate to go ashore and slice off some bark from the shadowy trees to which the boat had drifted.

Captain Jack studied the bark a moment. "I know them trees," he grunted. "Them's the cottonwoods on John Markey's place. The cottonwoods in front of his stable. We're in good shape now. Full speed ahead."

In a fog, said legend, the graceful cranes, then so numerous on the river, were particularly useful to a pilot. The cranes, as every Mississippi-dweller knew, were old steamboatmen, reincarnated so they could stand all day in the water and watch the paddlewheels churn foamily past. When fog had blotted out river and shore, to guide their old associates they would fly ahead of an oncoming boat to a snag or a rock that might send it to the bottom. They would rest there until certain the pilot had seen the danger, then would fly slowly on to the next obstruction, until the pilot could bring his vessel safely into harbor.

"Plenty of times I've had them cranes take me home," said Captain Jack. "Mile after mile."

Every steamboater, whether captain, pilot, mate, or lowly deckhand, possessed a profound sense of humor, always close to the pilot house and the perils of the river. As the boats drifted between the sunbaked levees or made a crossing under the jeweled stars there were long, uneventful hours to let the pilot's fancy wander; he would drawl out some tale from the rich river treasury.

"The captain of a boat was looking for a pilot," Captain Charley would begin as the cabin boy brought us coffee. "Three pilots came wanting the job. The captain asked the first one if he knew the river.

"The pilot swelled up like a turkey cock. 'Captain, I know every foot of this river. I been running her ten years and I ain't ever hit a snag or grounded on a sand bar.'

"The second pilot stepped forward and the captain asked the same thing—if he knew the river.

"This second pilot was a sort of solemn fellow. 'Captain, I could run your boat blindfolded,' he says. 'I been piloting on this river thirty-two years and I ain't ever touched a snag or a sand bar in my life.'

"It was the third pilot's turn and the captain asked the same question he'd asked the others.

'Do I know the river, Captain?' this fellow answers. 'Captain, there ain't nobody alive knows this river like me. 'Cause I've hit every snag and turned over in every eddy and been stuck on every sand bar she's got.'

"The captain put out his hand. 'You get the job,' he said. 'You really do know the river.' "

I was standing watch one morning with Captain Charley when we passed a wrecked steamboat, lying like the bleached skeleton of a prehistoric monster on the sandy shore.

Captain Charley studied the wreck with sardonic eyes.

"Everybody can make a mistake except a steamboat pilot," he said. "A bookkeeper can rub out his mistakes with an eraser. And a doctor can bury his. But a pilot puts his mistakes right out where everybody can see."

The crew of a steamboat usually formed a tight-knit community. But wherever individuals work in close association there spring up feuds arising from mankind's basic perversity. The feuds on the river had a particular savor. There was the continuous feud between the pilots and the engineers. When the landing was bad the pilot blamed the engineer for his delay in answering a signal; the engineer, sweating at his throttle, cursed the pilot for his clumsiness.

Blue Johnny was on a boat once with a pilot noted for his constant bell-ringing and his temperamental steering. The boat tied up at the wharf of a little town and the crew started ashore for a few hours' holiday. All except Blue Johnny. Instead he began dashing wildly about the engine room as though he had been seized by a fit, now sending the engines into half-speed, now suddenly throwing them into reverse, then frantically pulling the levers forward once more in a giddy full-speed-ahead.

The captain, hastily summoned, looked on in alarm. "What you doing, Johnny?" he demanded. "You going crazy?"

In answer Blue Johnny threw the engines into a violent reverse again. "Ain't doing nothing," he exploded. "Just trying to catch up with all them signals that so-and-so of a pilot give me so I can be finished with 'em before we get to the next landing."

But surpassing all river feuds was the conflict between the steamboaters and the shantymen living on their little houseboats along the shore. The feud began when the waves from the first paddlewheel sent the nearby shantyboats into a frenzied dance; many a shantyman's meal was lost when a frying pan full of mouthwatering catfish went flying from the stove into the river. The usual pilot would slow down when he neared a shantyboat. But at times a sportive-minded steersman would race past with the throttle wide open and watch with delight as the shanty

bobbed like a cork up and down in the water. I knew of several
pilots who had received a bullet in an arm or a shoulder as a
reward for their playfulness.

The *Tennessee Belle* was docked one day at Vicksburg, taking
on cotton, and I had stepped aboard the shantyboat of a grizzled
old river-dweller nearby, when a towboat went speeding past,
churning up waves that rocked the shanty as though it were in a
hurricane.

My shantyboat friend shook his fist at the disappearing vessel,
cursing the pilot and several generations of his children. When
the waves and his temper had subsided, he spoke to me quietly.
"You fellows off the *Tennessee Belle* are all right," he said. "That
there Captain Dick'll slow down when he passes a shantyboat. But
them other fellows is just plain mean. They'd laugh if they
drowned you." He chewed the plug of tobacco I had brought him
in meditation. "I'll tell you how it is with them kind of pilots.
You warn 'em twice to slow down. You give 'em fair warning
twice. And the third time if they don't slow down it's according to
the law to shoot 'em."

At times there were bullets of others than shantyboaters of
which the captains needed to be wary. Moonshiners were everywhere, particularly up the less-frequented tributaries. Once Captain Dick happened to be named an honorary recruiting officer
for the United States Marines; in token of his appointment he was

presented with a large Marine flag. Proudly Captain Dick flew the banner where all could see from the flagstaff in front of the *Belle*'s pilot house. All went well until the boat was called to bring down some cotton from the White River in Arkansas, noted as a paradise for illicit whisky-makers. He entered the river and was rounding the first dark-forested bend when a bullet crashed through the pilot-house window. In a moment more rifles cracked and bullets whistled from behind every tree.

Some hardworking moonshiners, busy at their still, had seen Captain Dick's new flag and decided he was a revenue officer.

The flag came down.

The Mississippi stern-wheeler was flat-bottomed as a packing crate—to which irreverent land-dwellers occasionally likened its entire structure—and could move in the incredible depth of three and a half feet of water. But at times even this slight depth was lacking.

I had come once more to the pilot house of the *Tennessee Belle*—on the same night I had first heard the melancholy call "No-o-o-o Bottom!"—when there was a sudden grinding under the hull as the boat scraped a hidden sand bar.

"River's tricky tonight," said Captain Charley. "Better take soundings again."

He blew a short blast of the whistle. A moment later the two leadsmen I had heard before appeared in answer to the signal. The giant black I had learned was called Chattanooga Jim; the dwarfish one was aptly named Bantam.

Chattanooga Jim moved to the bow and picked up the measuring line; Bantam took his previous post on the texas a few feet in front of the pilot house.

Chattanooga tossed the line into the black water and quickly drew it toward him, then threw back his glistening head. "O Mark F-o-u-r!" he chanted in a voice poignant with its old melancholy. "O Mark F-o-u-r!"

Bantam turned his wiry body to listen. From his upturned head there came an echoing call in a sobbing tremolo: "O Mark F-o-u-r! O Mark F-o-u-r!"

Captain Charley's cigar glowed in the darkness. "Four fathoms. Plenty of water. But I'm not trusting it for a minute."

The giant Negro at the prow swung the lead again. "Quarter Less Three!" he chanted. "Quarter Less Three!"

"Quarter Less Three!" echoed Bantam at the pilot house, his voice throbbing like a violin string about to break. "O Quarter Less Three!"

"Sixteen and a half feet," announced Captain Charley. He gave me a cigar.

I smoked with him in silence while the boat moved on slowly. In quick succession there came the calls, "Half Twain," "Mark Twain," "Quarter Less Twain," with always their quavering echo. Suddenly there came a sharp cry, "Five feet!"

Captain Charley gave the bell cord to the engine room a violent jerk. The paddlewheel churned foamily. There was a new, harsh grinding along the bottom. The *Belle* shuddered and came to a halt. The asthmatic sighing of the smokestacks quickened. The paddlewheel churned in desperation. Great Niagaras of water poured from its enormous blades. The *Belle* shivered like a frightened animal and was free again.

"Close one," muttered Captain Dick, who had come up from the shadows.

The shoal ended. The croaking of the frogs in the willows alongside grew fainter as the shore glided swiftly away.

Chattanooga Jim cast the line again. "No-o-o-o Bottom!" he chanted. "There is No-o-o-o Bottom!"

"No-o-o-o Bottom!" echoed Bantam.

The little black man joined the burlapped giant below. They started to move across the deck.

Captain Dick called after them, "Good singing, boys. Tell the cook to give you what you want to eat."

The *Belle* steamed into the starry blackness.

But it was not all picturesqueness which made up the life of the steamboatman. For the river was ever ready with some new grim trick; in an instant a peaceful afternoon could change to stark tragedy. I have been standing at the bow of a vessel moored to the bank in the quietest water when without warning some mysterious current seized the hull and wrenched it violently. The heavy boom above me supporting the gangplank smashed into a tree and fell a few feet from my head, hurling the mate and a dozen shouting black men into the water. I have been a cub beside the pilot when a hurricane blew up from the Gulf, and have watched the vessel sweep out of control, while the pilot house, attached only by frail guy wires, quivered and a thousand times seemed about to topple into the swirling water. I have been on a steamboat in the floods that race down the Valley till the earth for miles was only a gray memory, and have watched the pilot, already exhausted from his Herculean labors, cheerfully take his vessel through new rushing waters threatening to overwhelm him, that he might bring food to the hungry and life to the drowning.

Like the sailor, the mountaineer, or any of those sturdy souls whose lives are spent at the mercy of the inconstant elements, the steamboatman was a supreme fatalist. Each time he took his vessel through a rain-swollen eddy and heard its ominous lapping against the hull, each time the lightning flashed in the distance and he drove his boat into a clump of half-submerged trees along the shore so that the towering hulk might have a feeble shelter from the oncoming storm, he knew well that this adventure might be his last. But he was a cheerful fatalist, as brave a figure as ever voyaged the waters of the earth, laughing in the face of the fate that would destroy him, loyal to his boat literally to his death.

They were truly a unique race these rivermen; when the last steamboat, the *Delta Queen,* no longer travels with her tourists between the hills of the Ohio and the levees of Louisiana on her way to New Orleans, America will never be quite the same. Whether captain or engineer, roustabout or shantyman, all were molded from the same Mississippi clay; they belonged body and soul to the river. The river was their God, their religion.

Their spirit was typified not long after the great Chicago fire when a stranger came to a steamboatman and solicited funds to rebuild the devastated city.

The steamboatman shook his head in stubborn disapproval.

"I ain't going to give you no money to build Chicago," he grumbled. "Chicago ain't never going to amount to nothing. It ain't on the River."

CHAPTER

ROLL
THAT COTTON

They are gone now, like the sweet-sounding whistles and the splashing paddlewheels. One day they were toting their huge bales of cotton down the muddy banks and the levees everywhere from the bluffs of bustling Memphis to the pungent warehouses of gay New Orleans. When they vanished it was like the dropping of a curtain at the conclusion of a tumultuous play, a signal that the old life on the river had ended. For the roustabout was as vital a part of a steamboat as the engine or the rudder; without him the steamboat was a mere wooden hulk, a creature devoid of life, helpless to perform its grave responsibilities.

There have always been in our history certain typical figures who evoke a whole era. A painting of a stern-browed Puritan walking grimly past the village church calls up all the troubled years of the founding of New England. The picture of a weary figure sitting behind his horses on the seat of a covered wagon recalls all the dangers and trials of the Western pioneers. The roustabout in his fragment of a shirt, his turban made of a flour sack, was the symbol of the steamboat era; the mere mention of his name conjures up visions of racing steamboats with flames leaping from their smokestacks and broad-hatted gamblers with pistols at their belts defrauding wealthy planters from New Orleans.

He was of a wonderful breed, a superb physical specimen, the pick of his race, at once the envy and the terror of his black fellows on the shore. Though generally born on a plantation, he had long since forgotten the days when he left his bandannaed mother working in the cotton fields to take his first job on a steamboat. In his new life he had nothing but scorn for the poor farm black man —and the sophisticated poolroom black of the city as well. He stole the girl or the wife of the black man on the land without compunction. When he put on the purple suit he had purchased for ten times its value from some tricky merchant in a country town, he was a dashing Don Juan no black woman could resist.

I was sitting on the boiler deck of the *Tennessee Belle* late one night, listening to the chatting of the roustabouts near me, some squatting on the splintery boards chewing tobacco or smoking

cigarettes, some stretched out on a mound of sugar sacks or in the warm space over the boilers they called the St. Charles Hotel. Beside me came a ghostly clanking as two other black men hurled great shovelfuls of coal into the glowing fireboxes; ahead of me came the steady, asthmatic coughing of the smokestacks.

The conversation grew spirited. They were great philosophers these roustabouts, always discussing something; now the subject had drifted to women.

"Don't ever git tangled up with no bossy woman," declared a runty little roustabout with a pinched face called Piece O' Man as he raised up from the tarpaulin where he was lying. "A bossy woman and a crowing hen always comes to a bad end."

The towering roustabout named High Pocket standing near him nodded in agreement. "And don't give no kind of woman a pair of shoes. The same day she gits 'em she'll walk away and leave you."

"I got married once," piped Chicken, a skinny roustabout with a squeaky, quavering voice that faintly resembled the cackling of a hen. "Couple of months before, a fellow sold me what they call a insurance policy and the day I got married I tore it up. 'Cause I knew if my wife found out she'd have killed me for it."

"You never can figure 'em," Piece O' Man called from the tarpaulin. "I knowed a rouster on the old *Ouchita*. He married a girl and she got mad when he started chasing other women and up and left him. A couple of weeks later he got a postcard from her in New Orleans with some kind of fancy writing on it. Couple of weeks later his head started getting stiffer and stiffer, and pretty soon it turned to stone. And then one night it fell off when he was sitting in a Memphis saloon. They got it in a show in Memphis now."

A carbide lantern gleamed brilliantly on the nearby shore. The boat blew a long, melancholy whistle. A moment later the mate appeared, a brawny, jovial man with a red shirt open at the collar. "Possum Point Landing coming up," he called. "Plenty of cotton waiting. Get going, boys."

In a moment the outstretched figures, as though by the flicking of a switch, were galvanized into action. The gangplank was swung loose and quickly dropped onto the bank.

For an hour the black men toiled by the flickering light of the lantern and the *Belle*'s great searchlight, rolling the bales of cotton down onto the boat. It was the height of the cotton season and the roustabouts were working incredible hours; there were no labor unions in those days on the river.

"Never get no rest on a steamboat," panted Piece O' Man, stopping an instant on his way up the bank again. "I had a friend, Half Dollar, died all of a sudden on a boat up White River. The doctor said it was 'cause he was five years behind in his sleep."

The work was finished at last. The *Belle* steamed slowly up the dark river.

The carbide lantern swung behind us and disappeared around a starkly silhouetted grove of cottonwoods that soon gave way to an endless line of willows. Lightning bugs flickered in phosphorescent waves over the water, now and then flying onto the boat; their glow seemed bright enough to read a newspaper.

The roustabouts stretched out again on their makeshift beds and began talking of their adventures on the river. Their accounts often took totally unexpected directions. To listen was a constant delight.

"Tell him about the time you took the mules to London, Chicken," called a vague figure from back in the shadows.

The skinny roustabout's bony face lighted. "It was what they call the First World War," he began. "They come to the river and asked us to go on the first boat bringing mules to England, 'cause they needed them mules mighty bad. It was a terrible trip and I figured we'd never git to the land again. But after three weeks we seen London ahead and the mate come down where we was working, gitting the mules ready to go ashore. 'Everybody git yourself shaved up and put yourself on a nice clean shirt,' he says. ' 'Cause the King of England's coming down to meet you, and he's going to give you a basket of fruit.' "

He thrust away a huge moth flown onto the torn sugar sack that formed his shirt. "We come into the harbor, and sure enough there the King was, a-waiting on the bank. He was a big, fine-

looking man, kind of like Captain Dick, with a gold crown on his
head so big they had a couple of people standing by him to push
it back when it got to slipping. He was holding a big basket of
fruit in his hands. And he give each of us a orange, a apple, and a
banana. He kept me there on the bank a-talking a couple of hours,
and I seen them fellows that pushed the crown gitting awful mad,
so I said I'd better be going. 'Don't you go, Chicken,' he told me.
'I want to keep you with me all the time. I ain't ever seen a fine
Creole black man like you before.' 'Course I told him right away
I couldn't. 'Cause I knowed Captain Dick'd git mighty mad if I
stayed away from the *Belle*."

Somewhere back in the stern of the boat a cow separated
from its calf mooed dolefully. Off on the shore a church bell tolled
solemnly. A new wave of insects swept over us, an invasion of
huge flying beetles that blundered heavily against the bales of
cotton piled nearby. We slapped at them blindly. The invasion
ended.

A new shadowy figure called from the St. Charles Hotel.
"Tell him about the church, Chicken."

The other's squeaky voice grew troubled. "Was somewhere down near Napoleon, Louisiana. Ain't never knowed just where and don't want to. Black fellow living down there asked me to come to church with him. Said it was a new kind of church, kind of like the Baptists or Methodists, named the Church of the Seven Brothers. I drives with him way out in the marshes, and we seen a little church and go inside. There wasn't no preacher, but instead the Seven Brothers was up there by the altar. And then I seen who the Seven Brothers was; they was seven big snakes longer than a rowboat and thick around as a whisky barrel. Some chairs is there in front by the snakes and we sit down for a couple of minutes and nobody says nothing. And then this fellow with me, seems like he's a deacon or something, stands up and says to the biggest snake, 'Daniel, is you asleep?'

"The snake shakes his head and the fellow with me kind of snaps his fingers. 'Come over here, Daniel,' he says. 'Come over here and git up in the gentleman's lap.'

"I see the snake kind of wink out of one of his yellow eyes and start towards me. And when he gits to my chair there ain't no lap to climb into. 'Cause by that time I'm back in Napoleon, that's thirty miles away."

Some gasoline torches showed on shore and I expected more bales of cotton. Instead it was a farmer with half a dozen hogs and some heavy farm machinery. I watched fascinated as the rousters avoided the fierce tusks that could rip a leg to pieces and brought the ugly animals aboard, the hogs emitting bloodcurdling squeals that would terrify hearers miles down the river. I watched with wonder as the roustabouts moved and lifted monstrous tractors as though they were children's models, pulled about by a string. Yet despite their enormous strength—I had seen one on a bet run up a steep hill with a 550-pound bale of cotton on his back—they often possessed a tenderness, a gentleness, that was remarkable. A bird with a torn wing, a dog with a broken leg, was sure to find a happy haven as their mascot on the boiler deck.

They would fight desperately—now and then fatally—at the

slightest provocation. Some went regularly to jail. Yet many were deeply religious. In the crew of the *Belle* three black men when not working as roustabouts were practicing ministers of the Gospel.

The farmer and his squealing and metallic cargo were safely aboard after half an hour. But the engineer found it necessary to remain moored to the bank for several hours to make some repairs. One of the rouster preachers, a heavy-muscled figure known as Gospel Jim, invited me to go with him to a little church in the nearby town, a favorite of the more religious roustabouts. A short walk across the levee brought us to our destination, a pathetic little church of the sort I knew so well, so poor that at night the preacher, before commencing a sermon, was always compelled to ask his listeners for money to buy kerosene to fill the oil lamp so the service would not be ended by darkness.

I took a seat on the dilapidated bench reserved for visitors. A middle-aged Negro went about taking up a collection. I made my contribution.

The preacher, a gentle, dignified old man, counted the result and shook his head. "All we got here is seventy-nine cents," he said wistfully. "Ain't there going to be nobody come up here and give us some more money?"

Not a soul in the congregation moved.

The preacher counted the collection again as though he might change the result. He grew more dejected. "All we got here is seventy-nine cents," he repeated, his voice quavering until it seemed almost a sob. "Ain't there going to be nobody come up here and give us some more money?"

Again the rows of figures sitting on the rough benches sat like black statues, silent, motionless.

The preacher counted the collection a third time, then sighed and shook his head again in resignation. "Well, if we ain't a-going to get it, I guess we ain't a-going to get it," he murmured. "I don't know what we'd a-done if it hadn't been for this precious gentleman sitting up here on the bench giving us a quarter. We'd have fell mighty low."

We returned to the *Belle*, where the engineer was still making his repairs. Each blow of his hammer echoed like a gunshot through the humid river night.

The conversation of the roustabouts, led by my companion, turned to religion. At the time education was uncommon among Southern black men; it was a rare roustabout who could read or write his name. Yet they sat for an hour discussing an involved chapter of the New Testament with all the intensity of medieval theologians settling the problem of how many angels could dance on the head of a pin.

At their request I explained reincarnation and then asked their preferences for an afterlife if the Hindu beliefs became reality.

Their answers were a poignant commentary on human aspirations in general and the long-suffering black man in particular.

"I'd like to be a peacock," declared Two Bits, noted for his ugliness. "Everybody looks at a peacock. They has such a pretty tail."

While his companion, Sixty-One, a sad-faced black man who

in his life had known only trial and pain, answered after long reflection that he would choose to be a milk cow.

"Nobody ever hurts a milk cow," he said. "All they does is pet her and give her all the hay she can eat, and blankets to keep her warm, and all the finest things there is anywheres. And when she gits sick, there's a doctor waiting right in the stable to give her some medicine. It'd sure be wonderful to be a milk cow."

One of the men near the boilers not involved in our discussion took out a pair of dice and began to roll them on the deck. The mood of the rousters changed violently. In a moment a dozen men had formed a tense circle about the dice-player. A rouster called Iron Man, an austere individual who served as deck boss, disappeared for an instant, returning with a pistol and a cigar box full of silver coins. Solemnly he took a seat on the deck, then set the box in front of him and laid the pistol at his side. I had witnessed this scene many times before. The roustabouts were inveterate gamblers; Iron Man was the banker and armed judge to arbitrate any disputes before they ended in murder. Soon the

47

dice were clicking steadily on the splintery boards; the men in the glistening black circle watched each throw with hypnotized eyes, as a rabbit watches the movements of a rattlesnake. The men rolling the dice would follow each throw with a rhythmic cough, like the hushed panting of the smokestacks. Another group started playing poker, the men murmuring hoarsely to themselves as they drew from the deck or slapped a tattered card on the packing crate serving as a table.

A few of the rousters, for lack of money, did not join in either of the games. Instead they began to talk of the hoodoo doctors who could provide them with a charm, known as a Tobey, to bring them good luck.

"Best hoodoo doctor on the river lives down at Hanging Dog Light," said Frenchie, a wiry, bright-eyed black man from the Cajun country. "Went to see him last year. His house was full of dried rats and dried monkeys and dried lizards and the window was so covered with spider webs you couldn't tell if it was night or day. Then he comes out, a black man maybe a hundred years old and so dried up for a minute you couldn't tell him from one of them lizards. 'Before I give you a Tobey you got to take what they call a physical examination,' he says. And then a black spider big as a washbasin comes sliding down from the ceiling and walks all around me, looking me over like a policeman looks at you when you're walking down the street after somebody's just robbed a bank. And he walks away and the hoodoo doctor says, 'Now I'll send for Jerry. Jerry'll give you the big examination.' Pretty soon the biggest rattlesnake I ever seen comes crawling through the door. 'Examine him, Jerry,' says the hoodoo doctor. And the snake crawls all around me, looking me over, jest like the spider.

'Now you got to let Jerry lick you,' says the hoodoo doctor. And the snake starts coming at me with his black devil's tongue clicking in and out of his mouth so loud it sounded like a mowing machine. I started getting out of that house fast. But the hoodoo doctor stops me. 'Where you going?' he says. 'Jerry ain't going to hurt you none. You can't git no luck unless you let Jerry lick you.' And then he told me all about the rousters he give Tobeys to and how lucky they was. 'Fellow named Ham Hawk let Jerry lick him all over,' he says. 'And next day jest walking down the street he found $100.'

'I wouldn't let that snake lick me for a million dollars,' I answers, and I go out the door. Guess that's why I'm sure the unluckiest man there is anywheres," he concluded sadly.

The rhythmic coughing of the men holding the dice continued, the rhythm varying a little each time the dice changed hands.

High Pocket near me watched the players intently. "I know that hoodoo doctor. Used to live in Vicksburg and he was always trying to git my tracks and spell me. If a hoodoo doctor can dig up your tracks with a shovel and put 'em in a hole in a tree he's got you. But I fixed it so he sure couldn't git mine. Whenever I passed the house he was living in I always dragged my feet."

"He's the strongest there is anywheres," added Piece O' Man. "If you shoot at him he'll catch the bullets and throw 'em back. And he can guess in three pounds of your weight."

49

A cold wind had sprung up suddenly and was whistling shrilly down the river. Almost at once a great sow came wandering over the deck. It was Clara, the *Belle*'s mascot, adopted by Captain Dick when she was a baby and now grown to elephantine proportions. The roustabouts petted her and moved aside to let her crowd in among them to share the warmth of the boilers.

"I got a mighty fine Tobey from that Hanging Dog fellow," added a light-colored rouster known as Mustard after they were settled again. "I kept it in my pocket and when I was drawing a card and it was a good one it wouldn't do nothing. But if it was bad it'd git all slippery and squirm like you was holding a snail. Now I lost it and I ain't got no money to buy me a new one."

"He'll give you a new one on what they call the 'Stallment Plan," declared Piece O' Man. "But look out if you don't pay the 'Stallment. Cause then the Tobey turns against you. I knowed a rouster worked on the *Chris Greene* out of Cincinnati didn't pay the 'Stallment and a week later he was in the crazy asylum. He thought he was a big tomcat and went around fighting every tom he seen and meowing everywhere for milk."

I went to bed soon after. The boat had stopped at a tiny settlement to take on cotton again. Beyond the cotton I could see a towering mound of sacks of cottonseed. The roustabouts, ever ready to break forth into some rhythmic chant that would lighten their strenuous labors, began to sing as they rolled the great bales down the muddy bank. The song was the roustabout favorite:

> *Captain, Captain, please change your mind.*
> *Take the cotton but leave the seed behind.*

As always their song was in a low minor key, vibrant with sorrow, a reflection of the black man's tragic history.

I fell asleep with the music in my ears.

I arose early and was on the boiler deck again with my roustabout friends when a great eagle flew overhead. Chicken, standing near me, watched it thoughtfully. "Eagle on the dollar was named Old Abe," he declared. "Use to carry messages in the War Be-

tween the States. They done got his skeleton now in the big museum in Chicago."

The conversation, thus begun, turned to birds and animals; I received new lessons in Unnatural Natural History.

"If you're walking out in the swamp and all of a sudden you smell watermelon look around you mighty quick," said the sleepy-eyed High Pocket, who had stayed up most of the night with the dice. "You're almost stepping on a cottonmouth'll kill you quicker than you can say preacher."

"A hundred times worse than a cottonmouth's a stinging snake," remarked Frenchie. "He's the worst snake there is. He's got a needle and a bobbin in his tail jest like a sewing machine. The pisen in him's so bad if he gits mad and stings a tree, in three days that tree's stone dead."

"Worst snake of all's the whip-hoop snake," added Piece O' Man. "He'll roll up behind you and before you know anything he's whipped you so bad you're ready for your coffin."

51

"Rather have all them snakes put together than a panther," declared Chicken. "A panther puts his paw in front of his mouth and throws his voice, just like that what they call a ventriloquist I seen in a show in New Orleans. That way you think he's coming from the front and before you know it he's making a hamburger out of the back of your neck."

As Clara, the pig, wandered back and forth, begging part of the roustabouts' breakfast, I learned how just before winter comes an alligator swallows a big chunk of wood so that the walls of his stomach won't grow together in his long hibernation. I learned from the rousters who had worked in the area where the river empties into the Gulf how the whale is so big and awkward he can't handle himself properly; he carries with him a pilot fish to steer him on his spouting way. Which is why you often hear of a whale going aground; his inexperienced pilot has made a bad mistake. I learned how spiders warn of approaching tragedy. Before President McKinley's assassination the spiders spun black funeral webs around his picture; before World War II, if you looked close, in every spider web you could see a capital W for war.

Their talk drifted off into ordinary history. Their interpretation was equally startling. "Guess you heard of this here Red Riding Hood," declared Frenchie. "Was England's biggest bandit. Robbed trains of millions of dollars and they never could catch him. 'Cause he carried quicksilver in his shoes."

Our conversation was interrupted again by the sight of a young black woman standing with a pigtailed little girl on the

levee, waving a battered umbrella. The pilot blew the whistle for a landing.

Piece O' Man shook his head wearily as he moved forward to swing the gangplank. "Doggone that Captain Dick. He won't just stop for people waving. He'll stop every time a horse waves his tail."

Behind the young woman and the little girl, however, was another mountain of cotton from a nearby plantation. The day was hot and the levee steep. Once a bale escaped from the hooks of Piece O' Man and High Pocket and started to roll down the slope into the river, followed by Piece O' Man's anguished cry: "Look out! Old Al's going to git it!" A cry that I had heard so often when it seemed that a bale was about to fall into the jaws of the mythical alligator who is king of the Lower Mississippi.

Piece O' Man's pinched face was strained with anger when the landing was finished and the boat, moving slower with its heavy cargo, chugged once more up the murky stream. "I'm going to git a new partner," he told me. "I ain't going to roll cotton with High Pocket no more."

But the incident was quickly forgotten. In an hour the two men—like all cotton rollers temperamental as ballet dancers—were devoted friends once more.

I was about to go to the galley for lunch when Turtle, a fat roustabout I had noticed was always at the nightly poker game, came up to me at the foot of the stairway. His manner was shy, his voice hesitant. It was obvious he wanted some kind of favor.

"Captain, I done lost all my money last night," he said at last. "Every time I play the cards I lose all my money. Please give me something to make me stop gambling."

Through a slight knowledge of the methods of witch doctors acquired after a long stay in Africa, I had gained a bit of a reputation among the roustabouts on the *Belle* as a beneficent hoodoo doctor.

"All right, Turtle," I answered solemnly. "I'll give you something to make you stop. But you want to be sure you really want to stop. Because when I get through you won't be able to play cards anymore."

"Yessir, Captain. I want to stop gambling."

That night in the dark of the moon I taught him this magical verse which I composed especially for the occasion. Spells in verse are far more powerful than those in limping prose:

> *Gambler's money is not for me.*
> *When I gamble my money rolls out to the sea.*
> *Set my hand to shaking*
> *When I sit down by the cards.*

When Turtle had mastered the verse, I told him that in the future, whenever he was about to play cards and looked at his hand he would see that it was shaking like willows in the wind. It was a safe conjuration. The outstretched hand of any normal human being shakes a little; the palm of a superstitious black man, I was certain, would shake violently. In addition, since a concrete object is vital to any authentic spell, I gave him one of the quinine capsules I carried as a preventive against malaria and told him to put it inside his hat. When the magic powder melted, I assured him, the charm would be in effect.

He went off happily.

I left the boat at Greenville next day and didn't return to the *Belle* until three months later. I hurried below to see how my client was faring. The other roustabouts were gathered in the usual tense circles gambling. But Turtle sat far away, watching with mournful eyes.

"How are you, Turtle?" I asked.

He shook his head gloomily. "Captain, I played cards twice after you put that there on me. And the third time it come over me all of a sudden. And I can't play cards no more."

Many times afterward he asked me to remove the spell, but with my inborn perversity, I never relented.

It's been a long time since I've watched a roustabout playing poker or rolling dice, with a deck boss like Iron Man sitting beside a box full of silver and a loaded revolver. It's been a long time since I saw a roustabout scatter bits of tobacco into the water to induce the all-powerful Old Al to smoke his pipe and thus create a fog so the boat would be compelled to tie up and the weary roustabouts would have a few hours' rest. And I am touched with a deep sadness, for I know that I will never see them again.

The roustabout was superstitious, spendthrift, shiftless; he was pointing nowhere and never arriving. In a world where mechanization and efficiency became the watchwords there was no place for him and his fellows; he could only languish and die.

But if there is a marine Valhalla where Old Al and Neptune and the other gods of the seas and the rivers preside over all good sailormen after their earthly time is ended, the Mississippi roustabout will occupy a post of high honor near the golden thrones. And a deep contentment and peace will spread over the gods and their lordly attendants and all who listen as he begins a plaintive chant:

> *Captain, Captain, is your money come?*
> *I jest wants to know, 'cause I wants to borrow some.*

CHAPTER

THE GOLDEN AGE
OF
THE STEAMBOATS

The day was hot, stifling. It was midsummer, and somber clouds were darkening the distant sky. Even in the pilot house of the little workboat *Ollie,* the air, despite the vessel's movement, was difficult to breathe.

My silvery-mustached friend Captain Matt at the wheel was talking about the old days on the river. "Yessir, it all begun the sixteenth day of December in the year eighteen-eleven, according to the history books," he said, puffing at a cheap cigar that shrouded him in a volcanic cloud of vile-smelling smoke. "That there's the day Robert Fulton started the paddlewheel of his steamboat going at Pittsburgh and steered her into the Ohio. He sure picked a wonderful time to try her out. Was halfway to New Orleans when he hit the worst earthquake ever come to this country. River'd get so wide one minute it was like the Atlantic Ocean and the next there'd be nothing but a dry hole big as the city of St. Louis."

"Lord fixed up that earthquake on purpose," said the mate standing near me known as Captain Jake, an elderly, graying figure like the pilot, but unlike the other with a considerable paunch uncharacteristic of rivermen. "He wanted to show the people what steamboating was going to be like after she got a good start."

A giant snag suddenly appeared just at the surface of the water ahead that could rip the bow apart as an ax splits kindling. Though the expression of his face did not change, Captain Matt's body grew tense. He swung the boat with a violence that sent an empty coffee cup standing near the wheel crashing to the floor. We chugged on up the river.

Captain Matt relaxed. "A earthquake was just right to show 'em. Ain't been a quiet day on the river ever since."

The oppressiveness of the air increased. The leaves of the geranium in a pot near the wheel drooped unhappily, like human beings in a desert for days deprived of water.

"Going to have a good storm," said Captain Jake. He took a sack of chewing tobacco from his pocket, and stuffing a handful into his mouth, munched it slowly. "Had hot times on the river with the flatboats even before the steamboats. Trouble with the flatboats was how'd you get back up river after you come down."

"Wasn't any trouble if you was smart like one fellow I heard of," declared Captain Matt. "He carried a old mule on his flatboat, and when he'd sold everything he'd brought down to New Orleans he'd sell the flatboat and ride the mule back."

He blew the whistle, a sharp, single blast. In answer an old black man, his face fringed with tufts of white hair, came into the pilot house, bringing us a pot of coffee. He was Uncle Gabe, who for years had been Captain Matt's cook on the workboats and was now, I learned, serving as his cook at home as well.

The old black man carefully took down three cups from a shelf and wiped them with a torn dishcloth. Slowly he filled them

with the steaming coffee and set them down before us; his movements were so slow, so rheumatic I could almost hear his joints creaking. He listened a moment to the conversation.

"All kinds of things come down the river in the old times," he said wheezily. "Pappy and grandpappy told me about 'em and I seen plenty myself when I was a little boy. There was store boats selling dry goods and junk boats buying old rags and bones and bottles and Indian fellows selling medicine to cure the chills and fever and dish boats selling pretty china."

He went about the pilot house collecting empty cups and set them on the tray he had brought. "There was crazy things, too. Once I seen a man riding the river on a plain old mattress all the way from St. Louis to where she empties in the ocean. And another time I seen a fellow traveling in a washtub with a couple of sawed-off clothes props for oars."

The hot sun overhead vanished as a heavy black cloud swept out from the distance.

Captain Jake looked out the window. "Storm'll be hitting pretty soon. . . . You made this coffee too thin, Gabe. Steamboat coffee ain't no good unless when you put a spoon in it she stands straight up. You try it yourself. When I stand a spoon in it she falls over."

The old man picked up the spoon and followed the other's example. He shook his head. "Sure ain't me, Captain Jake. It's the coffee. Coffee ain't what it used to be old times."

He took the tray with the empty cups and went outside.

Captain Matt ran the boat close to the cypresses that fringed the shore. "These is good trees to tie up to if the storm gets bad." He spun the wheel again and turned to me. "Talking about old times, you ever hear of the steamboat *Big 'n Plenty?*"

"Not that I remember."

"Well, you ought to. Was run by old Captain Auter up the Sunflower River at Vicksburg before the war between the Rebs and the Yanks. Wasn't no steamboat at all at first; her engine was a bunch of wild Irishmen pulling big handlebars that turned a paddlewheel. Eighty of 'em, working in two shifts, forty each, and they was holy terrors. Every chance they got the two shifts'd start fighting and Captain Auter'd tie up and let 'em go at it on the shore. When a couple of dozen fellows was laying cold on the ground the others'd throw water on 'em and they'd all shake hands and go on up the river."

He blew the whistle in answer to a towboat traveling swiftly downstream. "But one trip they was fighting every minute and when they come back to Vicksburg Captain Auter hurried down to the boatyards. 'Get to work on my boat right away,' he told the foreman. 'A busting boiler ain't half as bad as them crazy Irishmen. I'm putting in steam.'"

Captain Jake sipped his coffee noisily. With a newspaper he slapped at a huge bumblebee driven by the threatening weather into the pilot house. "Them was the days all right. Steamboats lined up at the St. Louis wharf for a solid mile. In New Orleans around five o'clock when everybody was getting ready to sail they made so much smoke it looked like the whole town was on fire. Fanciest things you ever seen the boats was; floating palaces they called 'em. Brussels carpets you'd sink in to your ankles and cut-glass doorknobs and chandeliers like I seen in the big hotel in New York when I went to the Odd Fellows convention. . . . Hope that storm ain't going to hit us before we get back to Vicksburg."

The black pall overhead broke into a hundred fragments with

edges of dirty white, like lace curtains hung too near a smoky chimney. The fragments dissolved into a solid mass again, blacker, more ominous than before.

A grim steel skeleton appeared on the shore ahead, a factory under construction to which we were bringing some building materials. We dropped off the barge filled with bricks and sacks of concrete we had been towing and prepared to return to our home port of Vicksburg.

We were moving out toward the middle of the river when we saw a figure waving frantically on the shore.

"It's old Captain Jesse Combs," said Matt. "Used to work on the snagboat. Lives on a farm just back of here. Guess he wants to go to town."

We touched land again and I watched the old man jump aboard with all the agility of a youth of twenty. A moment later he was in the pilot house and I saw him closely, a quick-moving little figure with crinkly eyes and crinkly, laughing face; he reminded the onlooker of a good-natured squirrel.

Uncle Gabe entered with more coffee.

The quantity of coffee drunk by Captain Matt and Captain Jake, like all rivermen, was phenomenal. As I took a new cup I remembered how once in the pilot house of a steamboat I began counting the number of cups I drank in the course of a day. I reached twenty-six and stopped counting.

Captain Matt offered our sprightly passenger a cigar. "We was talking about old times," he said.

The other accepted the cigar quickly and popped it into his mouth as a hungry squirrel does a chestnut. "Couldn't talk about nothing better. Wish they was back."

Captain Matt nodded hearty approval. "Pilots got a thousand dollars for just one trip up the Missouri. Steamboats making so much money one of 'em had a deck on her all covered with white sand so it was like one of them fancy beaches down in Florida."

"One captain I heard of paid fifteen thousand dollars just for a gold-and-silver water cooler," said Captain Jake.

Captain Matt looked dubious. "Guess the water cooler was all right, but I ain't so sure about the water. It was the same as the kind Old Barney on the *Tennessee Belle* used to drink, pumped right out of the river. Only difference was they put a loaf of stale bread inside to kind of make the mud settle faster."

The storm struck suddenly, with a vivid flash of lightning that seemed to set the black sky afire, much as the flames leap through the smoke of a burning oil well. Captain Matt sent the boat into a new grove of cypresses. The single white deckhand on the bow below us made the lines fast to some gnarled cypress knees. The wind moaned despairingly through the branches overhead. We sat waiting until the storm would subside.

"Talking about drinking water," said Captain Jesse, puffing at his cigar. "Maybe Barney and them others was right. Captain I knew was running a boat and one of them state health inspectors come around to tell him he'd have to start using filtered water. The captain was six foot two and built like them brewery horses you used to see in St. Louis. He turns on that inspector like a tiger. 'Look at me!' he roars. 'I been drinking this water all my life. Do I look sick?' And then he calls in his five sons, all whopping fellows bigger than him. 'Look at these boys. Do they look sick? When the blankety-blank governor of this state can show me his family as healthy as that I'll put in your filtered water.'"

For an hour we remained snugly in the trees while the rain fell about us in drops so large they seemed like transparent marbles. The drops changed to hail, big as crab apples. They

struck the deck with a rattling sound like volleys of rapid-fire rifles.

As we waited the three old men continued to talk of the earlier days on the river. I heard how a wife would often accompany a captain on his trips, crocheting the days away as she sat in the prim ladies' cabin. I heard how the widow of one captain could tell by putting her finger in the vapor issuing from a valve whether the steam was "wet" or "dry"; if it were dry there was too little water and the boat was liable to explode.

"Boats I wouldn't have wanted to be on was them temperance boats," declared Captain Jesse. "Biggest was the three they called the Christian boats, the *Golden Rule,* the *Golden Crown,* and the *Golden Cross.* Couldn't dance on 'em, couldn't drink or do any kind of gambling. Their captains was big church people; they figured if you done any of them things you was selling your soul to the devil."

"The temperance boats missed plenty with that no gambling," declared Captain Matt. "Was mighty big business on the river. Friend of my granddaddy's got paid sixty-five thousand dollars a year for the liquor and gambling business on his boat and didn't even guarantee he'd make a single trip."

"They was real sporty fellows, them gamblers," added Captain Jake, searching for something on the shelf. "Dressed to kill, just like you seen 'em in the movies. And busting with tricks. One fellow used to always play in front of his stateroom, where a pal of his'd be sitting in the doorway pretending he was reading a paper. But he was really watching the transom; he'd tilted the glass so it showed all the cards of the men the gambler was playing with, just the same as if the gambler was holding 'em in his own hand. Then if the fellow watching scratched his ear or rubbed his eye the gambler'd know the man he was playing against had a straight or a royal flush. . . . What'd you do with them indigestion pills, Matt? I can't find 'em nowheres. These storms always makes my stomach worse."

He turned to me in explanation. "Rivermen always has bad

indigestion. Guess they just got too many things worrying 'em."

The search was successful after a moment. Captain Jake swallowed the pill noisily.

The storm lessened. The howling of the wind ceased. The lone deckhand jerked the lines free. The boat continued on its way down the water.

A mass of twisted iron showed ahead, part of a bridge washed down in a flood. Captain Matt gave it a wide berth.

"Plenty of hull inspectors with this low water," observed Captain Jake.

Captain Matt nodded. "They're bad this year. Be lucky if we don't knock a hole in our bottom. . . . I'm getting like Jake was saying, doing too much worrying. Maybe I'm getting too old for piloting."

"Ain't the getting old," commented Captain Jesse. "It's the times we're a-living in. Old days you didn't have near so much bothering you. Didn't have no railroads or trucks to take all your freight. Make enough one trip pretty near to pay for building your boat. And if things was bad the gamblers come in real handy. Wasn't anything for a gambler to lend a captain five thousand dollars. Then some night, when maybe the gambler'd got into bad trouble, like maybe some planter'd caught him with five aces, the captain'd land the boat out in the woods and let the gambler get away."

"My dad used to tell me a gambling story," added Captain Matt. "Swore it was true, but I don't trust no riverman. Even my own father. Two crooked gamblers tried to bribe the captain of a big boat to let 'em start a game. The captain kept on saying no and the gamblers kept on raising the ante higher and higher. Finally they offered him ten thousand dollars. This time the captain got real mad. 'You fellows get off my boat right now,' he said. 'You're getting too close to my price.' "

Vicksburg appeared ahead. The boat, like a hungry horse nearing its stable, went faster. We landed soon after.

The clouds overhead had thickened once more. But the lull

in the storm continued. We had docked near *Big Mama,* the giant towboat of the Mississippi, the famous towboat *Sprague.* But no longer was she pushing her barges that stretched row on row up the river; now like a female Samson shorn of her power, she was grounded forever on the riverbank, an outdoor museum to be gaped at by awestruck tourists. We sauntered over and I looked again at her enormous wheel; I had last seen it one unhappy night from the pilot house of the *Tennessee Belle.* Her giant waves had broken up our tow and caused us to struggle blasphemously until dawn and all the next day, collecting our wandering barges from the cotton plantations and the stagnant cypress swamps where they had drifted.

There came a new shower of hail. We scurried onto the great towboat for shelter.

"Never was no boat like her anywhere," said Captain Jesse as we stood in one of the white-painted doorways. "She could haul don't know how many trainloads of freight all at once and then come a-crying for more."

"They says she never did let her paddlewheel go all the way," declared a grizzled figure in overalls who like ourselves had taken shelter from the icy avalanche. "If she had she was so big and powerful she'd have broke up every building along the shore, even if they was a mile away."

I looked out onto the Vicksburg landing, once crowded with

steamboats. I could see again the dramatic events that had transpired here: the Yankee gunboats bombarding the town and forcing the starving residents into surrender; the steamboats rushing the panic-struck men and women up North to escape the deadly yellow fever.

"Some mighty fine boats landed here," declared Captain Matt. "And some mighty fine captains, too. Like Captain Leathers of the *Natchez* and Captain Cannon of the *Robert E. Lee*."

"That Captain Leathers beat 'em all," put in Captain Jake. "One day he seen a young fellow that was a passenger whittling at the railing of his new boat. He doesn't say anything, just gets a big knife in the galley and begins slashing the young fellow's fancy suit.

'Hey! What you doing?' says the young fellow. 'You're cutting my coat!'

"Captain Leathers takes another good whack with the knife. 'Yes, sir! Damn it, sir! You're cutting my boat!' "

"First searchlight on a Mississippi steamboat mighty upset things around here when it come down the river," said Captain Matt. "Happened the same time there was a big comet and people along the shore run every which way thinking it was the Day of Judgment. They figured the searchlight was the eye of God, picking out the good people from the bad."

We waited patiently for the storm to subside again. I heard

my companions tell how in the older days the steamboat whistles were valued by their owners even more than by Captain Dick of the *Tennessee Belle* and his fellow steamboatmen of my own time. They would be handed down from boat to boat as treasured heirlooms, just as a wealthy collector might bequeath to his children an ancient tapestry beyond price or a dazzling jewel which had once belonged to a king. I learned how the huge bell at the bow of a boat which was rung just before it left the wharf was similarly revered. Sometimes a captain would throw two thousand silver dollars into the molten iron when a bell was being cast to increase the beauty of its tone.

I heard how in the Golden Days of the Steamboats everything began and ended with the river. The crews of the boats, spending their hard-earned money in the towns where they landed, created a lusty, roaring life whose traces are still evident today.

"Wasn't nothing you could think of a steamboat wouldn't carry," said the grizzled man. "Even a whole circus. Boat carrying a circus sank somewheres up near Memphis and a big lion swam onto a island where some Holy Rollers was having a revival. When that lion dripping wet stood roaring beside the preacher they says more people got religion from them two than Billy Sunday and all them other shouting sky pilots put together. . . . Looks like the storm's slackening. Hope that hail ain't ruined my cotton. I'm owing too much right now to the bank."

He disappeared up the wharf.

Patches of blue appeared overhead; soon the last gray cloud drifted off to the horizon. The air grew fresh, invigorating.

We left Captain Jesse, and walking to Captain Matt's car, found Uncle Gabe already there, dozing in the back seat. Quickly Captain Matt drove us to his little frame house overlooking the river, where Uncle Gabe was to continue his duties as cook and Jake and I were to stay for dinner. The walls were covered with pictures of steamboats of an earlier day, piled so high with bales of cotton the vessels themselves were almost invisible.

I asked the exact date of this Golden Age. My companions

couldn't agree. Probably the peak was the ten or fifteen years before the War Between the States and a lesser peak the fifteen years after. But there could be no disagreement as to the causes of the steamboat's decay. Chief reason was the railroads, winding their steely way ever west and south.

In the post of honor among the pictures was a gaudy print of the *Robert E. Lee* and the *Natchez* belching volcanic flames and smoke on their bitterly fought race up the river. I asked Captain Matt if he knew anything of this famous contest, which more than anything else symbolizes to America the era of the steamboat.

His silvery moustaches rippled with a smile. "Come back in the kitchen and talk with Uncle Gabe."

The old black man was peeling potatoes for our dinner, with a little black girl, obviously a grandchild, busily acting as a helper. His white-tufted face brightened as he learned the reason for our visit.

"I sure does know about that race," he said. "My grandpappy seen it and my grandmammy seen it and when I was a boy there was still roustabouts around worked on the *Lee* and the *Natchez* both."

He cut a long curling peel from a potato as carefully as a sculptor carving a delicate statue. "It begun way back there when Abe Lincoln and Jeff Davis got to arguing about having slaves and things. Pretty soon Jeff Davis wanted Abe to fight him, and Abe said, 'If you want me to fight you got to git me mad first.' So Jeff hit him, and Abe says, 'You ain't hit me hard enough.' And then Jeff hits him a second time, and Abe says, 'That ain't hard enough, either.' And then Jeff hauls off and hits him a whopper pretty near knocks him to the floor, and this time Abe's shaking all over. And he says, 'Now you really got me mad. Now I'm going to kill you.' And then they had a fist and skull fight, and then the big war begun. . . . Susie May, git away from that stove before you burn yourself to a cinder."

He waited till the child had moved out of danger, then selected another potato from a dishpan and repeated his careful surgery. "General Lee was the general for the South but he lost the war and was feeling awful bad. And Captain Cannon seen him in Natchez that way one day and Captain Cannon says to him, 'Don't you do no more worrying, General. I'm going to build the prettiest boat was ever on the Mississippi and I'm going to name her for you.' Well, General Lee says he'd like that fine and Captain Cannon gits the boat built up in New Albany in Indiana, that's on the Ohio River, round about 1870, that's five years after the war's over. And the painters was just starting to put her name on her, *Robert E. Lee,* in letters big as a house when the New Albany people find out about it. And they're all Yankee people, done fought in the war, and they git torches and things to come and burn her down. But Captain Cannon's too quick for 'em, and he takes her over to Louisville on the Kentucky side of the river. And there's plenty of Rebel people there and they paint the name on her in a hurry. And they didn't have no more trouble."

"Them Yankee people sure liked to burn things," said Captain Jake. "Look at the way Sherman done Atlanta."

Uncle Gabe didn't notice the interruption. "Well, seems like there was this Captain Leathers had a pile of boats, same as Captain Cannon, and he heard about the *Lee* and it made him wild, 'cause he hated Captain Cannon way a king snake hates a rattler. Both of 'em come from Kentucky and when Kentucky people hates they hates terrible. And Captain Leathers says, 'I'm going to build me a boat that'll outrun that *Lee* boat so fast her engines'll git all choked up with the muddy water my boat throws on her. And I'm going to call my boat the *Natchez* 'cause there was a tribe of Indians named Natchez and I always liked Indians.' And then he builds the boat up in Cincinnati and they pass each other in the river down near New Orleans. And Captain Cannon makes his family go inside 'cause he don't want 'em to hear Captain Leathers cussing, he says Captain Leathers cusses so bad."

"He was a pretty good cusser," said Captain Matt.

Uncle Gabe pulled the child away from the stove again. "Well, the boats meets at New Orleans and everybody starts talking how they're going to race, and betting stacks of money high as a house. Both the captains puts ads in the paper the day they're leaving saying it ain't so, there ain't going to be any race. But all the time they're sweating rain barrels full running around gitting the boats ready. Course all the people knows about it and you could have robbed every house in New Orleans 'cause everybody in the whole town was down at the wharf waiting. But there

wasn't nobody robbed 'cause all the burglars was there too. At five minutes of five the *Robert E. Lee*—they called her the *Wild Bob*—backs away from the wharf and it ain't till three minutes later that the *Natchez* gets to moving. And a cheer goes up from the *Lee* people you could have heard over in Florida. But the colored folks ain't cheering 'cause they was just out of slavery and they sure don't want the *Lee* to win."

He began cutting the potatoes into chunks for a stew. "Well, the boats go up the river, the *Lee* gaining a little more, and around one o'clock in the morning she passes Baton Rouge, and now the *Natchez* is ten minutes behind her. And Captain Cannon is dancing a jig on the deck, he's so happy. And just that minute a black fireman comes running up to him from the engine room. 'The boilers is leaking terrible, Captain. Ain't hardly any water left in 'em. Engineer says if we don't put out the fires she's going to blow up sure.'

"Captain Cannon gits white as a ghost and runs down to the engine room. 'We'll let her blow up before we put out the fires,' he tells the engineer. 'We'll blow up everybody on this boat.' "

"He'd have done it, too," said Captain Jake. "Way I heard he'd have sat a roustabout on the safety valve of the boilers or anything before he'd lost the race."

"That's jest the way Grandpappy said," agreed Uncle Gabe. "Well, the engineer didn't want to git Captain Cannon mad. And he didn't want to git blown up neither. So he wraps hisself in gunny sacks and gits the firemen to pour buckets of water over him, and then when he's like a wet sponge he crawls down in the ashpit under the boilers that's still full of red-hot coals. And he lays there till he finds the leaks, and comes out with his hair all smoking, looking like the captain was gitting him ready for a big barbecue. And he chops up a rope into little bits and puts 'em in the water going to the boilers. And it stops the leaks and she goes on full steam again. She gits to Natchez Under the Hill in the morning and all the people watching there's feeling terrible, 'cause the *Natchez* is ten minutes behind her. And then she gits to Vicksburg, and now the *Natchez* is eighteen minutes behind."

He put the pan with the potatoes on the stove. "Well, every town they pass the crowds git bigger and bigger. Captain Leathers on the *Natchez* made 'em take all the fancy hams she had hanging in the galley for the passengers and throw 'em in the fireboxes so the fat'd burn hot and give 'em more steam. And all the country people living along the banks smelled the smoke coming out of the stacks and smacked their lips and said, 'I'd sure like to git some of that fine frying ham. That's sure wonderful ham.' "

Captain Matt interrupted again. "The *Natchez* burned ham all right. But wasn't the passengers' ham. Was condemned ham the people owned stores in Natchez gave to the boat to make the race."

The old black man shook his head stubbornly. "That ain't the way I heard it. But all the burning don't do no good. The *Natchez* can't catch up no way. When the *Lee* gits to Memphis next day the *Natchez* ain't in sight nowhere; she's a hour and four minutes behind. And then the *Lee* gits to Cairo and the *Natchez* don't git there till a hour and ten minutes later. And then the *Lee* sees St. Louis up the river and the people riding her go plumb crazy. And there's excursion boats and ferry boats and all kinds of boats come to meet her. And there's so many ladies waving their handkerchiefs on 'em it looks like the boats has wings. And all the bells in the church steeples is ringing so loud I guess plenty of 'em cracked. And then the *Lee* hits the wharf nice and easy and a rouster on her holds up a flag for the *Natchez* to look at, though she sure can't see it 'cause she's way down the river. The flag says, 'Shoo Fly. Don't Bother Me.' And the race is over."

"But the arguing sure ain't," said Captain Jake as we braved the twilight mosquitoes and moved onto the porch. "*Lee*'s time from New Orleans to St. Louis was three days, eighteen hours, and thirteen minutes. But there's plenty that say if the *Lee* hadn't got coal barges waiting for her in the middle of the river so she wouldn't have to land to refuel, and if the *Natchez* hadn't stopped

for cargo, the *Natchez*'d have beat the *Lee* hands down. If you're looking for a good fight right now all you got to do is walk around Natchez and say the *Robert E. Lee* won."

"Was the railroads really come out the winner," added Captain Matt. "St. Louis people had a banquet for both boats and all the big fellows come and made speeches how the race was sure going to make things wonderful for the steamboats. But I guess the dishes wasn't even washed when Captain Cannon that same night sent a telegram to his agent that was expecting him to come right back to New Orleans, saying instead he had to lay up the boat. There wasn't enough freight to make the trip. The railroads had got it all."

We sat down to dinner soon after. Night fell. The weather had changed violently again. The air grew warmer. A heavy fog began to settle over the Valley.

We ate and talked of the race once more. The mist thickened, becoming one of those impenetrable Mississippi fogs that made every tree beyond the window a brooding giant and every bush a gloomy phantom.

"Glad I ain't out there on a boat tonight," said Captain Matt. "It's things like that made them old-time rivermen always have indigestion. Just the same as Jake and me."

A towboat whistle sounded in the distance, quavering mournfully across the shrouded hills.

Uncle Gabe came in to bring us coffee. The whistle sounded again, sadly, like the cry of a lost soul seeking a final resting place.

The old Negro's eyes grew dreamy. "There'll be a-plenty of them whistles tonight," he murmured. "Grandpappy used to say when you heard them whistles in a fog it was the ghost of the *Natchez* trying to beat the ghost of the *Robert E. Lee*." *

* Uncle Gabe's account of the origins of the Civil War is slightly at variance with the beliefs of most historians. He is similarly mistaken in one aspect of the Captain Cannon–Leathers feud. The *Natchez* was built first and the *Lee* later, not vice versa as related by Uncle Gabe. In the details of the race, however he is astonishingly accurate.—B.L.B.

CHAPTER

OH, I'M
A SHANTYBOATMAN

There aren't many left. But if you look hard up some forest-bordered stream or remote bayou you can still find one hidden in a quiet cove. Maybe if you're lucky you can come on a whole little community. Exactly how many there are nobody knows; not even Saint Christopher who looks after foolish wandering writers and gypsies and tramps.

When I was spending my days on the river I estimated there were thirty thousand, scattered all the way from St. Paul and Minneapolis to New Orleans and Pilottown in the Jetties where the muddy river empties into the blue Gulf. This was a wild guess, based on my many journeys among them. I doubt if there are a tenth of that number today. There has never been any census of shantyboatmen; the census is government and shanty-boaters don't like government. That's the reason they are shantyboaters. They are the original rebels, the perfection of rugged individualists. If a shantyboater saw a census-taker approaching, he would be certain the visitor was a revenuer come to look for a hidden still; or at the very least a truant officer seeking to drag his children off to school, where they would be forced to sit at a desk all day, instead of being on the river watching the white cranes fly against the sky.

"Whenever the blue jays begin hollering in the spring I got to start moving," declared Buttereye Jim as we stood in front of his shantyboat moored beside a levee on the Mississippi near Memphis. He was a dignified-looking old man with snowy white hair and snowy white beard. The worn black suit he was wearing, with its long, dilapidated jacket and fraying black trousers, made him resemble a small-town undertaker whose business was failing. "I'm so poor I couldn't buy a racing jacket for a cricket," he continued. "But I'm like my rooster in that coop back of my shanty. He's always got his feet crossed, ready to go."

"I'm the same way," said Hominy Ike, a lean, hairy man as he scratched the head of the dilapidated hound at his side. "I'm always ready for traveling. I got fifty-three pieces of baggage. That's fifty-two pieces in my deck of cards, and the fifty-three's a bar of soap."

"If you ain't too busy with all your fancy traveling come down to my shanty," put in a tall, rangy individual called Catfish Johnny. "I'll give you some of them pork chops I traded on the bank for that twelve-pound buffalo I caught this morning."

We walked along the levee a few hundred feet to Catfish Johnny's shanty lost in a clump of cypresses, and went inside. The floating cabin, like most shantyboats, contained only the barest essentials for the life of a river nomad: a sink, a table, a few boxes that answered for chairs, and a crude bed with a woebegone hound, a perfect twin of the dog of Hominy Ike, dozing underneath.

The walls, however, made up for any lack of luxury or artistry. Every inch was covered like wallpaper with pictures cut

from magazines and newspapers. There was never a greater lover of art than the Mississippi shantyman. By the window was a gaudy print of a great ship sinking into the sea with hundreds of hands stretched out of the water in desperate supplication. Beyond it was a calendar bearing the picture of a barefoot boy sitting sadly beside a sick dog, with the printed announcement overhead stating that for any emergency the best drugs could be purchased at the Excelsior Pharmacy, open every night till ten o'clock and six on Sunday. Next to a Sunday-school picture of Jesus driving the money changers from the Temple was the lurid cover of a *True Detective* magazine.

Everywhere about the cabin were chairs in various stages of construction. Catfish Johnny was a practitioner of that ancient craft of the river which probably came down from the Indians, the art of willow-weaving. Out of the branches of the willows growing everywhere along the bank he would fashion chairs to be used in the summer kitchens and porches of the houses in the neighborhood.

He had finished his cooking of the pork chops and was setting them on the table when his son entered, a serious young man with brilliant red hair and once blue overalls that were mostly patches. Loaded down with several empty wooden boxes, he let them fall with a clatter to the floor.

Catfish Johnny hurried over for a quick inspection. His angular face grew gloomy. "Doggone, these here's all Florida orange boxes," he said. "All the time you been bringing me them Florida orange boxes. Can't you find me no California orange boxes?"

The son shook his head. "Ain't nothing anywhere but the Florida orange boxes, Pappy. California orange boxes ain't come in yet."

Catfish Johnny's gloom deepened. "Doggone, I don't know what I'm going to do if I don't get some of them California orange boxes."

I discovered that he used the wood to bottom his chairs; the California boxes made much better seats.

"Talking about Florida," Hominy said to Catfish Johnny. "You ever been there?"

"No, I ain't."

"I been there plenty," Hominy continued. "Miami, St. Petersburg, all over." He added with a note of pride, "I was in Jacksonville longer than anywheres. I was in the new jail there the day it opened."

We sat down at the table and ate the pork chops with gusto.

It was early winter and the shanty was growing cold. Catfish Johnny shoved some driftwood into the broken stove and struck a match. He looked quizzically at Hominy Ike who was rubbing his hands over the leaping flames. "I see you ain't wearing no overcoat this year."

Hominy Ike shook his head. "I can't afford no overcoat with the price of whisky as high as it is."

We sat talking of the river and of the people who made up the little community of perhaps a score of shantyboats. Catfish Johnny, like so many of his neighbors, was a Tennessee mountaineer who had succumbed to the lure of the city, and arriving at last in Memphis, had obtained work in a factory. But soon he rebelled against the thundering of machines and the punching of time clocks. Finding some planks on a sand bar, he had built a shantyboat and taken up his home on the river.

There is no life so free as the life of the shantyman. There is no rent to pay and no interest on a mortgage; there is no water or gas meter in your cellar ticking away your hard-earned pennies by the minute. For water you need only dip a bucket over the side; for fuel pick up the brush along the shore. When you're hungry bait a hook and catch a catfish. If it's fresh vegetables that you crave, the last three rows of a cornfield or potato patch along the river by tradition always belong to the shantyman.

A graying, middle-aged man in a shabby suit walked slowly down the bank and disappeared into a nearby shanty. "That's Skimmer Jim," said Catfish Johnny. "They took his wife off to the lunatic asylum couple of weeks ago. But he couldn't get in. He couldn't pass the examination."

"Sure been some funny people around here," added Buttereye Jim. "Guess about the funniest was Whistling Jack. When his nets didn't catch no fish he'd take a switch and pretty near beat 'em to death. If they'd be full when he pulled 'em in he'd pet 'em like a mother does a baby."

"Queerest one way I figure was Old Paul, the atheist," declared Hominy Ike. "He'd climb up to the top of a tree in the middle of a terrible storm, and with the lightning flashing all around him, dare God to come down and strike him dead. Sometimes he'd tell God he wished he had Him in his rowboat so he could shove Him overboard and drown Him."

Some neighbors drifted in and took seats on empty boxes, two unshaven men and a woman wearing worn black stockings.

Suddenly Buttereye leaped to his feet, and running to the window, looked out at the swirling river. "Things is a-coming down!" he shouted.

The effect of his words on the others was electric. Excitedly

they rushed to the window and pressed their faces against the glass.

"There comes a fine barrel!" cried Catfish Johnny.

"There's a wonderful table!" called his wife, a cheerful, blue-aproned little woman who had come through the door a moment before.

"And look at that there box!" shouted one of the newcomers, a gaunt figure wearing a battered sombrero. "Can't ever tell what you're going to find in a box!"

They all scurried out the door. Leaping into their rowboats, and seizing their oars, in an instant they were darting over the yellow water, in feverish pursuit of the treasures bobbing on the waves.

They returned soon after, loaded down with their spoils. For this is another advantage of being a shantyboater. The river is the shantyman's department store; best of all, everything is free. For anything can drift down the current: a picnicker's canoe broken loose from upstream, with a basket of sandwiches and a wonderful bottle that keeps coffee hot for hours; or a lady's coat with huge mother-of-pearl buttons. If it is high-water time, the prize may be a cotton bale or a kitchen pantry full of groceries or even a fine piano.

"Ain't too many things coming down now with low water," said Buttereye. "River's so low I seen a catfish swimming upstream had a bullfrog going ahead of him taking soundings."

Most of the men were chewing tobacco, but Catfish Johnny and the black-stockinged woman were smoking corncob pipes. The shanty was shrouded in an acrid veil of smoke when Buttereye jumped up from his seat and rushed out the door.

I asked Catfish if his friend had suddenly become ill.

"Ain't sick noways," Catfish chuckled. "He jest hates the smell of tobacco mighty bad. So every time he's in a place where there's plenty of smoke he goes home to wash out his beard."

I left the shanty now and walked with Hominy Ike and his dilapidated hound along the river. Several of the shanties we passed had fenced-in rafts where scraggly chickens were parading, with a chicken coop beyond.

Hominy Ike studied the strutting birds as we passed. "Know how a owl steals a chicken?"

"No, I don't."

"He gets into the coop at night when all the chickens are asleep and knocks one of the hens down from where she's roosting and eats her in a hurry. Then he flies up and takes the hen's place. Pretty soon the rooster wakes up and counts his hens to see there ain't any missing. In the dark he figures the owl's one of 'em so everything's all right. And then he gives his first crow, that's the counting crow, and goes back to sleep. And the owl slips out the way he slipped in and when the sun comes up he's gone."

"I didn't know an owl was so smart."

A calico mother cat was sitting beside a shantyboat, surrounded by five frolicsome kittens. "Smart? They're ten times as smart as that cat. A owl can count up to twelve. But a cat can just count up to three. If you took away two of them five kittens the cat wouldn't know no difference, 'cause there'd still be three left. But if you took three away that'd just leave two and she'd tear you to pieces. . . . You know how to steal a chicken yourself?"

"I haven't stolen one lately."

"You want to know how?"

"There aren't always restaurants around. I might find it useful."

"I'll tell you the best way. First thing you pick a real cold night. It won't be no good unless it's a real cold night. Then you go into the coop and pick out the row of the best-looking chickens and put your arm right by where they're resting. Your arm's plenty warmer than the cold air in the coop. So one by one them chickens moves over onto you. When you got seven or eight fat ones sleeping on your arm you get out of the coop nice and easy." He chewed his tobacco thoughtfully. "Fine thing about it, you ain't really committing no crime. You ain't committing no sin at all. 'Cause it's the chickens deciding. Ain't you."

We neared Hominy Ike's shanty, and joined by his next-door neighbor, a towering individual with skin weather-beaten until it seemed like leather, went inside. The interior was even less pretentious than the dwelling of Catfish Johnny. But the decorations

were equally elaborate. On the walls hung gaudy-colored photographs of two young men, one standing before the shanty with his sporty hat cocked jauntily to one side, the other bareheaded and somewhat older, sitting with a girl at a table in a cheap restaurant.

I asked who they were.

Hominy Ike's hairy face lighted with pride again. "Them's my sons," he answered. "The one with the hat on's my youngest. He's a mighty fine boy. Right now they got him in jail for a while for breaking into a house. The other one's my oldest. He was a fine boy too. He was killed by a policeman in Dallas."

"I got three boys myself," added the weather-beaten visitor. "And I been mighty lucky with 'em. I sure been mighty lucky. They're all three living. And they all been in the penitentiary. But ain't one of 'em had the straps put on him to be electrocuted."

Hominy Ike showed me his other treasures: a piece of a milk bottle colored blue by the sun, sent to him by a friend who had traveled to Arizona; a sea fan from Miami; a present given him by a shantyman who had worked a short time in the nearby hospital—a bullet taken from the chest of a wounded gunman who had held off fifteen policemen.

He took out a box carefully tied with faded red ribbon. "This here's the best thing I got. It's the teeth all my people before me's had pulled. Back as far as my grandpappy's pappy." He lifted the lid of the box, exposing perhaps two hundred yellowed teeth of all shapes and sizes, and took out several to show me. "This here one belonged to my pappy's brother they called Cross Cut. This here one belonged to his sister. I'd sure hate to lose that one. It's got gold in it. This here one's the best, I guess. Ain't many of them kind around. It belonged to Pappy. And it sure give him a time getting it out. It's a three-pronger."

I took my leave and finding my car, drove over the nearby bridge into Arkansas. Following a country road that ran close to the river, I came on another shantyboat colony, a little larger than the one over which Catfish Johnny presided, set along the edge of a dense cypress forest. Not far away were the ruins of a once prosperous factory where mussel shells brought by the shanty-boaters were turned into buttons.

I dropped in at the shanty of an old friend, a small, shriveled man known as Little 'Bama, who looked as though he had fallen into a vinegar barrel and had not been pulled out for several days. He greeted me warmly as did his dog, of the same woebegone variety as the other dogs in shantyboat society.

"How are the ha'nts?" I inquired. Little 'Bama's attraction for ghosts was famous along the river.

"Woods is getting so full of 'em they're crowding out the rabbits," he answered. "One was pestering me yesterday. Walking up and down outside my shanty all day. Couldn't see him but I could see the puffs of dust he was kicking up every step. The dog seen the dust too, and followed right behind him. Then all of a sudden I seen the dog give a jump and start hollering something awful. And I knew the ha'nt was whipping him bad."

Twilight fell, bringing with it scores of mosquitoes; their stings were like poisoned needles applied by some demoniac torturer.

"Mosquitoes is terrible this year," said my host. "Yesterday I seen a mule kick a stone to make a spark and start a smudge fire to keep 'em away."

It grew dark soon after. We ate a catfish Little 'Bama had caught a few hours before. In the reflected light outside the window I could see an old raccoon, attracted by the smell of the fish, coming closer and closer to the shanty. At last be began scratching noisily on the door.

Little 'Bama shouted at him to go away. "Ain't going to fool with raccoons no more," he declared. "Used to always have one around as a pet. But not after what they done to Bill Tatum couple of days ago."

"What'd they do?"

"Got him put in jail, that's what. Bill'd just run off some moonshine, and there was a lot of mash by the still. Raccoons love moonshine mash and maybe fifteen or twenty of 'em come and ate it in a hurry. They got so drunk they was staggering around and falling down like a bunch of sailors ain't been in a saloon for a year. And Bill's bad luck, just then a revenuer come along and seen a couple of them raccoons going down the bank and stopped and smelled their breath. It was so bad if you'd struck a match they'd have blowed up like one of them manhole explosions when they got a gas leak. 'Course it was easy as nothing to track the coons back to where they'd got drunk."

The raccoon outside made indignant guttural noises and began scratching imperiously on the door again.

Little 'Bama picked up a bucket of water, and opening the door, hurled the contents in the direction of the black-masked head.

The raccoon scurried off into the bushes.

Little 'Bama shut the door. "I ain't making whisky right now but I'm liable to any minute. I don't want that raccoon a-spying on me."

"How long did Bill get?"

"Six months way I heard yesterday. Making and possessing. 'Course it ain't the first time he's been in that Helena jail. He's been there so often they keep the same number for him every time he comes back."

There was a knock outside and a gaunt, lanky shantyman known as Corporal Jeff entered, accompanied by two hounds that looked as if their forebears antedated the Indians and had mixed with every race and tribe of dogs come to America ever since. But though the lineage of the pair, called Amos and Andy, was doubtful, their talents were startling. Corporal Jeff was on his way to hunt possum and invited me to go along. Out in the forest with my own eyes I saw Amos and Andy, when they thought they had spotted their quarry, expertly climb trees. I admit the trees had gnarled and twisted trunks that here and there provided a faint foothold; they were not pines soaring straight into the sky. Nevertheless they were trees, with all a tree's difficulties.

As I walked with Corporal Jeff through the somber woods I

learned more Unnatural Natural History of the sort I had acquired from the roustabouts I learned, and to this day I don't
know the truth, how a raccoon catches crabs with his tail. Dan-
gling the tail in the water, he patiently waves it back and forth; the
crab thinks it some new delightful kind of fish and nips it with his
pincers. Before the poor slow-witted creature can let go the coon
whips the tail onto the shore with crab attached—and has a gourmet dinner. I learned about the porpoise who swims in the Gulf
and the brackish waters of the Jetties. If a porpoise finds the body
of a man floating out at sea, he will always blow it into shore so
it can have a Christian burial. For the porpoise many eons ago
was a man himself and has never forgotten his humanity.

"Them porpoises ain't the only ones picks up floaters," said
Corporal Jeff. "Sailor from the Coast Guard come along the other
day and said I'd picked up more drowned people than anybody
on the river. There's a fellow down in Vicksburg says he's picked
up more than me, but don't nobody listen. He's just a show-off.
Sometimes you can make a pretty good living with them floaters."

His face grew troubled. "Caught a floater about five years ago
I thought was sure going to make me rich. He was one of them
big fellows had a factory or something in Little Rock and his fancy
cruise boat blowed up when he was taking some ladies out on the
river. Was a friend of the Governor and the Little Rock paper
said the Governor'd give a reward of five thousand dollars to anybody found the body. All the shanty people and everybody was
going crazy looking for him but was me that found him. I went all
the way to Little Rock to get the money. And all they give me was
fifty dollars instead of five thousand. They said the paper had
printed it wrong. They'd left off the dot in the middle. Course I
knew they was lying. You can't trust them politicians noways."

Despite an elaborate search—to my private delight—my companion could find no possum. With the dejected Amos and Andy
trailing behind we made our way back toward Little 'Bama's
shanty.

As we neared the settlement, another shantyman joined us,
a burly individual known as Paddlefoot Bob, who was returning
from a similar vain hunting expedition. We crossed a footlog
serving as a bridge over a little stream. A shadow that might be an
alligator showed a short distance away.

"Saw a whopper of a 'gator here last week," said Paddlefoot.
"So big if a steamboat seen him they'd have blowed a passing
whistle."

"I seen a fight here a while ago between a 'gator and a loggerhead turtle," added Corporal Jeff. "The loggerhead licked the
'gator in five minutes. Bit off one of his legs easy as a kid breaks
off a chunk of peppermint candy."

"Loggerhead'll do it every time," said Paddlefoot. "That's

why there's so many three-legged 'gators around. It ain't Old
Al. It's the loggerhead that's the king of the river."

"Any kind of turtle's the strongest thing there is," declared
Corporal Jeff. "I killed a turtle one time when I was living on
the land and cut off its head and throwed the head in my chicken
yard. Three days later the head went snapping around and killed
every chicken I had."

We passed a shanty where by the light of a kerosene lamp
a giggling young woman was sitting at a table, serving coffee to a
smiling young shantyman.

Corporal Jeff turned to me. "That's Joe Jessup's widow. Joe
got married since you was here and then all of a sudden up and
died. While he was dying he said to his wife, 'After I'm dead you
be true to me or every time you ain't I'll turn over in my grave.'
Soon as they buried him she begun running around with every
pair of pants in the place. Now we call him Whirling Joe."

We were in the heart of the colony now. We neared a shanty
nestled snugly under a great cottonwood.

"Old Uncle Asa Eggers is mighty bad off," said Corporal Jeff.
"We better go in and see how he's doing."

We went inside. An old man wearing a pair of cheap glasses
was lying in a crude bed, afflicted with some wasting disease.

"You ought to let 'em take you to the hospital, Uncle Asa,"

said Corporal Jeff with surprising tenderness as he prepared some coffee. "Ain't right for you to stay all by yourself this way when you can't get up or anything."

"I'm all right. Getting better every day." He drank the pungent liquid gratefully. "I ain't going to leave the river for no hospital. Here I can lay and look out and see everything coming up and down the water. If I left the river in no time I'd be dead. . . . Give me the Book over there by the window, will you, Jeff?"

Corporal Jeff gave him the worn Bible lying on a chair.

The old man wiped his chipped glasses and pored over the fraying pages. "I ain't never had no learning. I wish I could read jest three words so I could see wherever they come in the Book— Lord, Heaven, Saviour. A fellow come through on one of them fancy houseboats and he marked 'em on a few pages and was going to do the whole Book, but the mosquitoes was too bad and he only stayed two days. Maybe you could do me a few."

I underlined the words on page after page until my hand and eyes grew weary.

It was time for us to go.

The old man sat up in the bed feebly. "Trouble is I ain't never been baptized," he murmured. "Tell that Holiness preacher down near Goldbottom Landing to come and baptize me, will you, Jeff? I don't want to meet my Maker if I ain't been baptized."

"They're having a Holiness meeting here at Aunt Callie Jackson's shanty in a little while," said Corporal Jeff. "That Goldbottom preacher's there already 'cause I seen him having supper. I'll tell him and maybe he'll come over to see you tonight."

We went out into the moonlight.

"State doctor come through here yesterday and said Asa ain't going to live more'n a few weeks unless we get him off the river. But ain't no making him go. One thing's kind of worrying us shanty folks. When we bury him ought we bury him wearing his glasses?"

We walked down the river a short distance to another shanty from which there drifted the shrill singing of a hymn, followed by the impassioned voice of a preacher. It was obvious the little

dwelling for the moment was serving as a Holy Roller church. We entered quietly and took seats on boxes at the rear. The stocky preacher was pacing up and down, sweating as though just emerged from a heavy rain. Luridly he drew a picture of the horrors of the hell to come and called on all sinners to repent before they were damned for eternity. His words were echoed by the congregation, interrupted every few moments by dolorous sighs and groans and a chorus of fervent Amens and frenzied Hallelujahs. The parishioners began to leap up and down in a sort of spasmodic dance until the boat rocked dangerously. They began to talk in tongues, a curious meaningless jargon they believed to be the Greek of Saint Paul, the Hebrew of Moses, and the Egyptian of Pharaoh.

The talking in tongues ended. The frenzy of the dancing increased. A young girl with black hair reaching almost to her waist suddenly leaped into the air. "Everybody that's got bobbed hair's going to die!" she shouted.

"Going to die!" chanted the congregation.

The preacher, who had been silent for a brief period, began his wild oration once more.

"What you going to do when the world's afire?" he shouted. "Where'll you be when the world's afire?"

The congregation echoed the question in a doleful chorus. "What you going to do? What you going to do? Where you going to be when the world's afire?"

There came a lull in the frantic ritual. Corporal Jeff spoke to the preacher about Uncle Asa, then went with Paddlefoot and myself out to the river again. A shantyboat was moored to a near-by tree. At the window we could see a cadaverous figure with an evil, degenerate face.

"Just come here yesterday," said Jeff. "He's a killer if I ever seen one. We don't like them kind around here. If he stays more than a couple of days we'll sneak up at night when he's sleeping and cut his lines, and when he wakes up he'll be twenty miles down the river."

"We'll do him the way we done them five Chicago gangsters come down a couple of years ago on a shanty and started getting tough. We lost 'em out in the swamp with the rattlers and the cottonmouths. When they come out they was so swelled up with mosquito bites you could have sold 'em for them six-foot pig balloons they sell for half a dollar at a carnival."

We stopped at the last shanty on the bank to see two other friends of mine, an old man and his wife, whose gentle faces were as wrinkled as the dried Spanish moss in the trees down the river. Like the shantyboaters we had just left they were very religious, though unlike the others they were not Holy Rollers. Devoted Baptists, they attended the church in the neighboring town at every opportunity. With sorrow they regarded the card-playing and drinking of their neighbors. In their minds the taking of a drop of alcohol was equivalent to the sale of their souls to Satan. Like their neighbors they could not read, but they had deep reverence for the printed word, particularly when concerned with religion. For a long time, above all else, they had wished for one of the framed religious mottoes so common in the rustic South. But their poverty had made such a priceless possession impossible.

"But we sure got us a fine motto now," the old man told me eagerly. "A wonderful fellow stayed here a couple of months give it to us. It says 'God Bless Our Home.' I'll show it to you."

He led me into the neat little bedroom adjoining. On the wall at the head of the bed hung the motto, resplendent in brilliant golden letters on rainbow-colored glass and framed with a shiny golden chain.

The old man's withered face beamed with joy. "It's a beautiful motto, ain't it?" he asked.

I studied the words a long time. "It's a wonderful motto," I answered.

The golden letters read simply: "Champagne Velvet Beer. The Best Beer in the Valley. Please Pay When Served."

We left soon after. Corporal Jeff and Paddlefoot walked with me to my car.

Corporal Jeff turned to me. "You ain't happening to be driving down to Helena, are you?"

"That's just where I'm going."

"Take Paddlefoot and me with you, will you? They're opening a new one of them fancy supermarkets there in the morning and they'll be giving away what they call free wienies."

"Them's wonderful wienies," said Paddlefoot. "Last time they had a opening in Sunflower me and Jeff each got seventeen. We want to get there early before they run out."

They climbed into the car. We sped gaily down the road.

CHAPTER

FISHBOAT

"You see funny things and funny people on a fishboat," said my companion. "Can't see 'em nowhere in the world I guess except here in the Black River country."

We were walking down the main street of the little town of Jonesville, in the heart of the tangled swamps of Northern Louisiana, the fish capital of the Lower Mississippi. All around us were tall unshaven men in high boots and ten-gallon hats come in from the surrounding countryside; the unfamiliar traveler could easily have imagined he had been suddenly transported to a cattle town in the heyday of the West. He might easily have believed he was surrounded by desperadoes eager to take his money and his life. Actually they were the kindliest of men, who liked nothing better than to joke with friend or stranger.

We reached the winding Black River where a fishboat called

the *Cocodra* was anchored, a small craft perhaps thirty feet long, its most prominent feature huge scales hung before the cabin to weigh the fish collected on its voyages. My companion, known as Little Breeches, was the boat's pilot, a quiet, small young man, not more than twenty-four, but with the weather-beaten face of one twice his age; he was wearing the same high boots and ten-gallon hat as the others. A brawny black man who served as the boat's combination engineer and deckhand was already on board awaiting our arrival. We joined him, and Little Breeches took the wheel. A moment later the black man started the engine. The boat swung into the seething current and headed down the stream. The nearby buildings vanished quickly; we had gone only a little way when I felt as if I were traveling along the Congo in the jungles of Darkest Africa. Everywhere the boat was surrounded by dark, brooding forests of pine and cypress, with long festoons of Spanish moss drooping from the branches; here and there a row of buzzards sat on a bough, like ugly sentinels.

A cabin appeared in a clearing ahead with a little dock at the water's edge. The *Cocodra*'s whistle snorted like an angry bull; the boat drew up alongside.

A towering figure in a Western hat came out to meet us. With the substitution of chaps for his tar-stained overalls he might have stepped out of a film where he had been the sheriff of the Pecos.

"That's Missouri Mike," said Little Breeches. "Best fisher-man on Black River."

Missouri Mike moved to a latticed box tied at the dock where some catfish and glistening buffalo were swimming, and began to toss them into the scales at the bow. When Little Breeches had noted the weight, the black deckhand tipped the scales and let the fish drop into the ice-filled hold.

Missouri Mike picked up a catfish larger than the others and held it up for Little Breeches to see.

The pilot examined it with interest. "How much you figure she weighs, Mike?"

The reply was instantaneous. "She weighs exactly a quart of whisky."

Little Breeches' serious face lighted with a smile. "You're a card, Mike. You're sure a card."

He put the fish in the scales and added its weight to the others. "You ain't done so good this trip, Mike. Ain't much more'n half last trip."

A trace of worry crossed Mike's unshaven face. "I run out

of P-and-G soap." He turned to me in explanation. "Fish is crazy as women. One year won't eat nothing but doughballs, bread dough with a little garlic in it. Next year they want turtle meat. This year they won't eat nothing but P-and-G soap."

A lanky figure with flaming red hair, who proved to be Mike's brother, came out of the cabin to join him. The newcomer, called simply Red, turned to the pilot. "Mike and me got to go downriver to see Tooter Scoggins about some hogs," he said. "Mind if we come with you?"

"Sure thing."

Both men strode aboard.

An enormous loggerhead turtle appeared swimming dead ahead of the boat.

Little Breeches swung away to avoid a collision. "Like to catch that fellow but ain't got time. I ain't had no turtle meat for a month."

"Turtle meat's best there is," commented Red. "Got every kind of meat on it, possum, coon, rabbit, cow, chicken. Doctors says even if you're in a hospital bed laying flat on your back and eat turtle meat you'll be up and dancing around quicker than a judge can say ten dollars."

We stopped to collect fish from two more grizzled swampmen, then neared a cabin that was obviously deserted.

The pilot glanced about searchingly. "Where's Cottonmouth Sam? In jail again?"

Missouri Mike nodded. "Went to Jonesville couple of days ago and got put in jail for being drunk. But he won't stay long. Church people'll get him right out the way they always do. When he's drunk he makes the finest temperance speeches of anybody in Louisiana."

The engine of the boat began to cough asthmatically, then stopped altogether. Little Breeches let the vessel drift to shore and with a long stick lying alongside the cabin poked out some branches snagged in the propeller. We chugged on noisily again.

Several more dwellings appeared, then a dilapidated cabin

where on the paintless porch a gray-bearded old man was sitting in a chair, dozing over a half-finished net he had been knitting.

He awoke with a start as the pilot blew the whistle, then with a dip net brought up a few small catfish from his fishbox and dropped them into the scales. A moment later he resumed his place in the chair and his drowsy knitting of the net.

"That's old Possum Meadows," explained Red, as we moved down the river once more. "Had a vision from a angel he was going to die when he was sixty-nine and just before his birthday he give away all his nets and furniture and things and waited up for the angel to come and get him. Course the angel never did come and the old man got awful mad and had a terrible fight to get the things he give away back. Now he figures he got the numbers in the vision wrong. He figures instead of the angel saying he'd die at sixty-nine he meant ninety-six."

I was learning that these Mississippi fishermen were characters, as individual and unique as the most colorful shantyboaters. Though farmers as well as fishermen, some were actually living on shantyboats as the cheapest and most convenient dwellings in the swamps. Like the shantymen and the roustabouts they were deep philosophers.

"Being a Mississippi fisherman's different than anybody else," said Missouri Mike as he chewed a fat cud of tobacco. "No matter what you do, like Possum giving away everything, it's your own business. Unless you go to crossing up your neighbors. Guess you heard about the fellows sell hunting dogs to people for plenty

of money but have 'em trained so the minute they ain't chained up they'll run back to their master and he can sell 'em over."

"I heard about them in Georgia."

Mike offered me a generous slice of his tobacco plug. I refused as gracefully as I could.

Mike put the plug back in his pocket. "There was a man here done that trick with the dogs and we didn't bother him none. We figured that was just good horse-trading." He spat with perfect accuracy at a drifting water spider. "But then a fellow come around was different. Was from up in Cairo, Illinois, he said. He done like the fellow with his dogs, only he done it with his wife. She was a pretty woman, good cook, too, and every new fisherman that come in here that didn't know nothing the Cairo fellow's wife'd pretend to fall in love with him, and the Cairo fellow'd say he was tired of her anyway and he'd let her go if the other fellow'd give him a good deal for her. She'd stay with the new man a couple of weeks, and then she'd say she was mad at him and go back to her husband. Well, we figured that was really crossing up your neighbors and we ought to do something. I ain't saying what we done. I'll just tell you he was a city fellow didn't like snakes. But you can bet he ain't coming around here no more."

Red agreed with emphasis. "Tried to get me to take her too, but I ain't having no more truck with any kind of woman. I had enough with my own wife."

He held out his arm on which was tattooed the name Nellie and a rainbow-colored heart. "She was a good fisherman. Fish come to her like ants to molasses. But she drove me crazy talking. Next time I get to New Orleans I'm going to a tattoo fellow and have her name took off me. I ain't going to carry that woman around with me all my life."

Little Breeches let me take the wheel now. Along the gloomy jungle we chugged slowly, stopping always to pick up more fish. Often Little Breeches would put off a sack of flour or a box of canned goods or a gaudy piece of furniture ornamented with

mother-of-pearl a fisherman had asked him to purchase in Jonesville; the fishboat was the sole link between the isolated swamp-dwellers and the bewildering world outside. So dependent on the boat were these remote swamp-dwellers, so clockwork-like the boat's trips, it served as the fishermen's calendar. Once because of an emergency the boat arrived on Wednesday instead of the usual Tuesday. Legend said that for months afterward all the Black River Valley was topsy-turvy; nobody knew the day of the week.

Occasionally as we traveled near the bank I could see a raccoon high in the trees or a great fish jumping before the bow. Once we passed close to a rattlesnake swimming steadily across the river, his head upraised, his beady eyes alert, menacing, ready to attack anyone trying to interfere with his watery journey.

We neared a narrow earthen mound, higher than the cabin of the nearby fisherman.

"That's one of the funny things I said you'd see on a fishboat," declared Little Breeches. "That there's a flood mound where the hogs and cows can go to keep from being drowned when you get high water."

Missouri Mike murmured agreement. "You get high water here in the Black River country pretty near seven days a week, including Sunday. This here's Mississippi overflow country. If it wasn't for them flood mounds wouldn't be no farm animals left."

"Wild animals get on 'em too," added Red. "Foxes, rabbits, raccoons, rattlers. And funny thing they don't fight neither. All excepting the wildcat. He's a worse killer than Jesse James."

Another cabin appeared ahead.

Little Breeches took the wheel to make the landing. "Now you're going to see something else. Heard about it last place we stopped."

I followed him onto the dock and stared in amazement. As a child, I had always thought of a catfish as a creature not much bigger than a herring. Here swimming in a wide-latticed enclosure was a monster perhaps five feet long and as thick through as a beer barrel; put on the scales it weighed 130 pounds. I learned that such a catch was not uncommon in the area; one weighing 250 pounds had been caught many years before.

We glided on through the moss-hung silence. We stopped for lunch at a shantyboat presided over by a birdlike little woman with bright blue eyes peering startlingly out of her fine-lined face. I heard how for years our hostess, known as Aunt Ettie, had lived alone in the watery wilderness, fishing and trapping; in her spare time she acted as letter-reader, midwife, and teacher for all her swamp neighbors.

"Things is sure a-changing," she remarked as she set some ham and steaming corn bread on the table. "People used to pay me a dollar a head to learn their children reading and writing. Now they come in boats to git 'em and take 'em to a regular school. Everybody says I could git a job quick in one of them schools. They says them teachers gits paid plenty more a head than I was gitting for learning 'em. But I don't like living around a town."

We moved on once more.

The river was full of snags and floating logs now. Little Breeches slackened our speed. But careful steersman though he was now and then the boat shook violently as it hit some obstruction lurking under the surface of the dark water. It began to list heavily as a leak developed in the wooden hull. Missouri Mike and his brother manned the battered pump. But the leak and the list increased.

"Better stop at Preacher Gibbs' and fix her up," said Little Breeches. "Preacher's mighty good at fixing a boat."

We passed some ancient cypresses, their twisted knees rising grotesquely from the swampy shore; they seemed like misshapen witches assembled for some evil ceremony. Beyond appeared a log cabin with several other buildings set around it in an uneven circle.

"Now you're going to see something else mighty different," said Little Breeches. "All them houses is built on Choctaw logs. Them are logs that's all hollowed out by Choctaw worms. When the high water comes, instead of having your house all flooded, the logs make it float and it raises up with the water. Then when the water comes down the house comes down with it, and you're back again in good shape, right where you started."

We drew near the little settlement. A half-dozen dogs came racing down the bank, yelping as if they were trying to rout a band of the river pirates who roamed the Mississippi country a hundred and fifty years ago.

"Them's Catahoula hog dogs," said Missouri Mike. "Glass-eye, leopard type. The finest dogs in the world."

The boat touched the bank and I had an unhindered look at the Catahoulas, who I had heard, just as Old Al was the king of the river, were the kings of the Mississippi swamps. They were sad, moth-eaten dogs, even more melancholy in appearance than the doleful bloodhound, bony as skeletons from their ceaseless chasing in the cypresses. Astonishingly their eyes were each of a different color, the right eye being pink, the left blue or vice versa; it was this characteristic which had given rise to the "glass-eye type" of Missouri Mike's description. The comparison to the leopard arose from their woebegone hides, mottled with spots of faded gray, acquired perhaps from some straying bird dog ancestor.

"Yessir, them's the finest and smartest dogs in the world," repeated Missouri Mike as we went ashore and the dogs crowded noisily about us. "Some say they ain't so pretty. Maybe so. But smart. Them dogs'd teach school or fly a airplane if you asked 'em to."

"That's sure right," added Red. "Fishermen couldn't live here without the Catahoulas. They'll find a rabbit or a possum for you if they have to go fifty miles; they'll warn you every time of a rattlesnake or a panther."

"Big thing, though, is his handling the hogs," declared Mis-

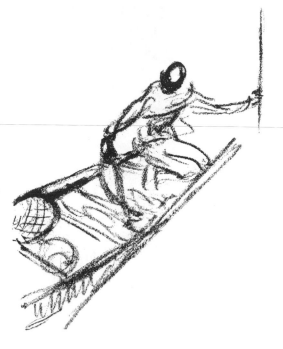

souri Mike. "Every fisherman here in the swamp has plenty of
hogs and every spring he puts 'em out in the woods to eat acorns
and things so he won't have to buy no feed. Then in the fall
there's a big hog roundup and the dogs go out and get the hogs
wherever they are, even if they're sitting up a tree. They drive
any hog they see into the nearest fisherman's pen, don't care whose
it is, until them woods is clean of hogs as a old maid has her
kitchen floor. Then the fishermen go and pick out the hogs in
the pens got their brands on 'em, and put 'em in their gas boats
and come on home. If I was a Arab and had four wives I'd trade
'em all in a minute for a good Catahoula."

Preacher Gibbs, who had been off in his garden hoeing corn,
hurried up now, a tall, somber scarecrow of a man, of a type that
had changed little since the first settlers had come into the area
shortly after the Republic's foundation. Instantly he set to work
with Little Breeches to put a patch over the leaking bow. When
he had finished, with the hospitality characteristic of the region,
he invited us into the house for coffee and a kind of hot corn

cakes. When they arrived, brought by his sad, sunbonneted little wife, both the coffee and the cakes were stone cold.

Preacher Gibbs apologized and pointed off to a little building a good city block away from which the refreshments had come. "That's the kitchen out yonder," he said ruefully. "With Choctaw houses you got to chain 'em to a tree when high water comes or they'll float away. Chain on the kitchen broke and she come down over by them trees. When the next flood comes we'll get her back at the house."

By now it was late in the afternoon. Preacher Gibbs suggested that we stay for the evening meal and spend the night. Little Breeches accepted with alacrity.

I went with our host for a walk around the little establishment. I found him a man of many talents. Besides being a preacher and farmer and carpenter he was an expert fisherman as well. On the riverbank in front of the cabin were several of the enormous hoop nets typical of the region, long woven cylinders almost high enough for a man to stand erect inside. The fishbox nearby was brimming with catfish and buffalo, swimming about gaily, unaware of their approaching doom. In a Choctaw stable were two horses and a cow; just beyond was a pen where a trio of pigs grunted contentedly as they ate corn husks. A score of hens, lorded over by a gay-plumed rooster, paraded about, searching for worms in the muddy earth. A fat scarlet-throated turkey stalked arrogantly up and down, like the Oriental pasha who had given it his name. There was no electricity, no running water, no comforts that existed in even the smallest town of the world outside; Preacher Gibbs was living as his ancestors had lived more than a century before.

Just beyond his property another cabin showed along the shore. We sauntered over, to be met at the door by a gnomelike old black man called Uncle Cash, one of the few but highly regarded black fishermen on the river. Like the dwellings of the shantyboatmen, the cabin was ornamented with every kind of decoration, shells of all varieties, and pictures cut from magazines. Over the fireplace, surrounded by fishing tackle, stood a huge cardboard portrait of a smug young American clubman advertising Arrow collars.

"Found him in a box full of trash in front of a store in Jonesville selling shirts and things," said Uncle Cash, looking at the picture with admiration "He's sure a pretty man."

We sat and talked until darkness began to fall, then prepared to take our leave.

The old man lifted a board in the floor and brought up two large blacksnakes. They curled about his arms with seeming affection.

"You wouldn't need no rat-catching done, would you, boss?" he asked me wistfully. "These here snakes is the best rat-catchers on the river."

We made our way back to the preacher's cabin. His pale wife lit a kerosene lamp, and setting the table, went out to get our supper. She returned not long after with the food stone cold again after its long trip from the wayward kitchen.

We finished the meal. Soon after, a score of unshaven men and aproned women drifted into the narrow room, fishermen and their wives from the nearby Choctaw houses. I quickly realized I was to witness another religious service. Preacher Gibbs' house, as so often was the case in the area, became the settlement's church. The service was similar to the Holiness ceremony I had attended at the shantyboat colony in Arkansas. But strangely, there was no music or singing. When there was a pause in the service, I asked the sunbonneted woman sitting next me the reason.

"This here's Christian country," she answered quickly, as though troubled by my question. "That singing and music ain't nothing but sin."

Her overalled husband next her nodded. "Them hymns makes you too happy. I used to sing them hymns good as anybody. But I sure stopped just in time. Them hymns ate me all up."

The service ended about midnight. Despite my protests my hosts gave me their handmade matrimonial bed. The other men stretched out on makeshift mattresses set about the floor.

I lay awake a long time listening to the symphony of the swamp, the hoarse, bass croaking of the giant bullfrogs and the shrill tremolo of their tiny brothers in the trees; the drowsy whirring of the cicadas and the rhythmic chirping of the crickets; the barking of nearby foxes, followed by the anguished barking and howling of the Catahoulas as they went off in hot pursuit; the eerie cry of a screech owl, like a ghost condemned to wander the swamp for all eternity.

I awoke at dawn and dressing quickly, found the others already sitting down for stone-cold bacon and eggs and potatoes and coffee.

"Did you hear them foxes and the dogs last night?" asked Missouri Mike, stuffing down his sixth egg.

I assured him the commotion would have been difficult to miss.

He helped himself to a new mound of potatoes. "Foxes in these swamps are the trickiest anywheres. Just loves to torment the Catahoulas. Works in pairs. One of 'em gets the dogs to run after him, and when that fox gets tired his partner takes his place. They'll keep it up all night. Then when neither of them don't want to run no more they sit up and lick their paws so the spit'll kill the scent and the dogs can't follow."

We boarded the boat again. Red looked back as the little

circle of Choctaws disappeared around a bend. "He's a fine fisherman and a fine preacher. Trouble is sometimes he gets people too excited. Couple of months ago they was having a Holiness meeting at his place and he gets 'em to telling their sins. And Ash Meadows stands up and says, 'Lord, I'm a terrible sinner. I done stole two fine fishing nets belonging to Jake Boggs sitting over yonder. Forgive me, Lord!" And Jake Boggs jumps up with his face all red and shouts, 'Lord may forgive you, Ash Meadows. But I ain't going to. Them was my two best nets. I'm going to kill you!' They had such a terrible fight a big panther been here in the swamp for years come around to see what was going on and got so scared he swam the Mississippi to get away and ain't never been seen since."

Constantly, as on the day before, we stopped to take on more finny cargo—the buffalo to be sold to unsuspecting New Yorkers as Russian sturgeon, the roe of the yellow catfish to become Russian caviar. Like the fish, the parade of picturesque characters continued. At one landing I met a grim, silent fisherman rumor said was a defrocked priest; at another a stiff-mannered, dark-bearded man with a foreign accent rumor declared had been a count in Germany, come to the swamps because of a tragic love affair.

A new Choctaw dwelling loomed ahead, larger than the others. The proprietor was standing on the dock, a heavyset man with a florid face and a permanent twinkle in his eyes.

"That's Tooter Scoggins," said Missouri Mike. "It's pretty near the end of the line. Here's where we'll be getting off."

The heavyset man greeted us jovially and hastened to carry

the wriggling contents of his fishbox aboard. He turned to the pilot with a grin. "You brought that wife you promised me, Little Breeches? I'm getting mighty lonely."

Little Breeches grew serious. "I ain't bringing no more wives. Just groceries. The women was either too young or too old, too skinny or too fat, too short or too tall. All I did was take 'em back."

Tooter chuckled. "Bring me a young one and if I don't like her after I've married her I'll do the way a young fellow I knew done up the Ouchita. Traded his young wife for his neighbor's old wife, a box of fish, a couple of hoop nets, ten head of chickens, and a good coon dog. . . . How's fish prices this trip?"

"Getting worse than ever. Looks like them people in New York's stopped eating."

The fish he brought filled the scales half a dozen times. When the last velvety-skinned yellow cat had slid into the hold, he invited us into his house for a drink. On the way I noticed two buzzards flying over a pen where half a dozen pigs were wallowing in the mud. "Them's my government hog inspectors." He chuckled again. "They come every morning to see how the pigs is doing. Then if any of 'em look sick they stay around."

In the house our host set a bottle of whisky on the table.

Missouri Mike took a long drink. "This here's good moonshine, Tooter."

"It's all right. But ain't what it was. Moonshine, music, women, ain't nothing like old times. Used to be when you throwed moonshine on a fire it'd go up in a flash. Now when you throw it on a fire it just kind of fries. That's the water in it."

We left our two passengers behind and continued a few miles farther down the river. Little Breeches swung the boat around and headed homeward. All day we traveled, picking up more fish at the cabins where we had stopped the day before. The finny riches in the murky water seemed inexhaustible.

Night fell. The boat moved steadily through the starry darkness. Now and then a pair of tiny green eyes showed in the black wall of trees along the bank where some curious possum or wild-cat warily watched our passage.

There was a glow in the sky ahead. Soon we were safely moored at the Jonesville landing. Our glistening cargo was trucked off to a packing plant, eventually to tempt the appetites of jaded New Yorkers to whom the simple fishermen I had visited were beings as remote as the headhunters of Borneo.

It was midnight now and the little town was almost deserted. Only a tall, wide-hatted, heavy-booted fisherman was about, pre-paring to return in his gasboat down the river. With him were two woebegone Catahoula hog dogs, slinking nervously at his heels. By the glaring electric light I could make out that each dog had different-colored eyes, the right one pink, the left one blue. I could dimly distinguish their faded gray spots left by some straying bird-dog ancestor. They were the authentic aristocracy of the Black River, the cream of the cream of the Catahoulas, the royal glass-eye, leopard type.

"Them's the finest dogs in the world," said Little Breeches.

You saw funny things and funny people on a fishboat.

CHAPTER

SHOWBOAT
ROUND
THE BEND

We strolled along the cobbled wharf of St. Louis. Huge trucks rumbled near us, loaded with chemicals and steel and machinery. From the flood-scarred warehouses near us came the pungent odor of roasting coffee and the acrid smell of new-made rope, relics of the days when the smoking stacks of steamboats had stretched as far as the eye could see. On the Eads Bridge above us a constant stream of automobiles was passing; under it the muddy river flowed sullenly like a great yellow snake that was the city's god and master, as its mood changed from tranquillity to violence, ready to aid or to destroy.

"Only a crazy man would run a showboat," said my companion. "It's like being in the Fun House at Coney Island. You never know when the floor's coming up to throw you flat on your face."

We reached the showboat moored at the shore. I had visited it many times before but I never stopped marveling at its fantastic design, traditional in the long history of showboating on the Mississippi. It was as if some mad architect had taken an old frame church from a tree-lined street in any American town, carefully cut off the steeple, then flattened down the peaked roof and covered the whole with white icing. At the completion it resembled something between an ivory cuckoo clock and one of those frosted Easter eggs with a window at one end I had so treasured as a child. For a final touch the lunatic creator had put his weird edifice on an enormous barge and launched it in the river. On the side of the vessel tall black letters proudly proclaimed its name, the *Goldenrod*.

"But I can't complain," my companion went on as we walked aboard and took chairs in front of the ticket window overlooking the river. "I've handled everything from a troupe of Oriental dancing girls to a devilfish twenty-five feet wide. The devilfish was easier."

My companion was Captain Bill Menke, famous along the Mississippi all the way from St. Paul and Minneapolis to the murky Head of the Passes that opens the way to the blue Gulf. In my time there had been a few other showboatmen—Captain Billy Bryant with his *Showboat* on the Ohio and Captain Cooper with his *Dixie Queen*—but none like my friend Captain Bill. As Captain Dick of the *Tennessee Belle* had been the last king of steamboatmen, so Captain Bill had been the chief Mohican of his dwindling tribe, the last king of showboatmen. Since the turn of the century he had been roaming up and down, buying a new showboat when the old one was shattered on a rocky dike or was squeezed to death in the grinding ice pack of a frozen river. Eighteen showboats and the steamboats which provided their motive power had once been his treasured property. Now he owned the last showboat left on the Mississippi.

Captain Bill shifted his stout body that made him resemble an all-year-round Santa Claus, and chewed the end of his extinct

cigar. He was in one of his usual talkative moods this warm June afternoon, and though I had heard his stories many times, I never ceased to delight in their retelling. They were a living history of the theater on the great river.

"Ordinary show business is bad enough," he began. "But when you combined show business and the river you were asking for terrible trouble. If it wasn't a drifting barge that crashed into you at night or a flood that cut you off from shore so nobody could come to see your show it was being stuck on a sand bar for a month with nothing to do but dodge water moccasins and catch catfish. I told you about the time we hit the snag, didn't I?"

"I'd like to hear it again."

His rotund body shook with reminiscent laughter. "It happened one night up on the Ohio near Pittsburgh. It was February, bitter cold, and we were just steaming out from the wharf when all of a sudden there was a terrible crash and I knew we'd hit something. I ran down in the hold and with my flashlight saw a big hole in her bow where she'd smashed into a piling. She was starting to sink and I knew if I didn't do something quick in a few minutes she'd be at the bottom of the river. So I jumped square into the break and plugged it with my body. I was even stouter in those days than I am now and my stomach fitted the hole exactly. I stayed in the freezing water a couple of hours while my brothers fed me whisky, trying to keep me warm, and the carpenter got a big patch ready. I felt like a living icicle when everything was over. But I was happy. Not a teaspoonful of water had got past me. My brothers said I plugged that hole so tight when they pulled me out I popped, just like the cork in a bottle of champagne."

A harbor tug chugged past, shrouding us in a thick black cloud as though it were laying down a smokescreen to hide us from an enemy. We wiped the soot from our faces.

Captain Bill lit a new enormous cigar. "Come in the office. I've got something to show you."

He led the way into the room behind the ticket window and carefully unrolled some lurid posters advertising melodramas which had been favorites on the river more than fifty years before: *Nellie, the Beautiful Cloak Model; Bertha, the Sewing Machine Girl;* and *Katy, the Moonshiner's Daughter.* Vividly they portrayed some harrowing scene from the play, the black-cloaked villain watching gleefully as the heroine, trapped in a lumber mill and bound like a trussed deer, is drawn closer and closer to the great saw whirling before her, or lies screaming on a railroad track while the *Chicago Cannonball* comes racing around the bend. These bills, I knew, had been of vital importance in the old showboat days. A bill-poster, called an advance man, would ride ahead in a wagon or car loaded with brushes and pastepots and put up his bills on every available fence or barn to announce the showboat's coming.

"Was a bill-poster myself when I was a kid," said Captain Bill. "For French's *New Sensation.* She was a big showboat before your time. A bill-poster had to go by himself in all kinds of places and you never knew what was going to happen. I was up the Cumberland River in the Kentucky Mountains, pasting up bills as usual, when a bullet went right through the bristles of the brush I was using. I raised the brush again and a second shot hit the handle. And then a third shot came and I figured I'd better get out of there in a hurry. I grabbed up my paste buckets and ran to my car and was climbing inside when a big mountaineer in overalls comes out of the bushes.

'Don't be skeered, brother,' he tells me. 'I ain't meaning you no harm. I ain't been so good with my shooting lately and the way that there brush goes up and down is as good as them jumping rubber ducks I seen in a shooting gallery once when I went to Louisville. I practices thataway with a bill-poster every time I kin.' "

"The mountains and a lot of the little places anywhere were rough on showboats," said Captain Bill's brother Harry who had joined us, a quiet, reserved individual in marked contrast to the exuberant Captain Bill. "If the people got an idea you had a belly dancer or anything they didn't like in the show they'd come down with axes and chop up your boat."

I had heard other showboaters tell of remote areas along the lower river or up the tributaries where such occurrences were not uncommon. To a Hard-Shell Baptist preacher a showboat, after all, was a theater on the water, and a theater was a deadly sin. Buying a ticket to a showboat was the same as buying a ticket to hell.

A young, unshaven figure, obviously from somewhere back in the Missouri hills, came slowly up the gangplank carrying a violin case. Captain Bill went to the open door.

The visitor stood silent a moment, hesitating. "You don't need no acrobatic musician, do you, Captain? I can play *Annie Laurie* on the fiddle same time I'm doing a somersault and *Dixie* on the flute while I'm swinging from a horizontal bar."

Captain Bill's genial face grew troubled. "Sorry, friend. We're full up. But if you're hungry go and ask the cook to give you a good feed."

The other disappeared in the direction of the boat's galley.

"The same now as it was a hundred years ago," said Captain Bill. "Every kid that could play a comb wanted to play on a showboat."

We talked about the older showboats: the *Floating Palace,* the *Water Queen, Price's New Floating Opera.* There had been some kind of floating theater on the river almost from the time the intrepid Robert Fulton brought his first Mississippi steamboat down the river. Competition was fierce as the different boats fought to be first at the important river towns like Memphis and Vicksburg and Natchez and New Orleans. If the advance man of one showboat found the posters of a rival already in a town he lost no time in tearing these down and putting up his own bills instead. Often a captain would try to trick a rival into going off on a false scent, billing a poor show town where he had no intention of giving a performance. When the rival had swallowed the bait and had anchored at the wharf of the unprofitable settlement, his wily opponent would steam off in a hurry to some favorable town where he was sure of numerous customers.

"Man I was always fighting was Captain Ralph Emerson had the biggest showboat on the Mississippi," said Captain Bill. "It was knockdown and dragout. No holds barred. His showboat carried a banner: YOU'VE SEEN THE MINNOWS. NOW SEE THE WHALE.

That got under my skin. But I fixed him up on the Monongahela, was the best showboat territory on the Western Rivers. The coal miners liked to see a show after being cooped up all winter, and the first showboat to arrive was always a sellout. I had my boat in dry dock one spring, getting some big repairs for my trip up North, when Captain Ralph happened to come along and saw the bad shape my boat was in.

He pretended to be sympathetic. 'Too bad the way they've got you in the hospital, Bill. Guess you won't be getting up the Monongahela this year, will you?'

'Guess I won't, Ralph.'

"I could see he was almost choking, he was so happy. 'Well, I'm mighty sorry for you, Bill. I'll be getting up there in a couple of weeks or so. Looks like it's going to be a fine year. I'll give 'em all your regards.'

"As soon as he was gone I got hold of the owner of the dry dock. 'How long did you say it would be before my boat's ready?'

'Two months. Not a day sooner,' he answered.

'I want her out in a week,' I told him. 'Hire every boatbuilder on the Western Rivers if you have to. But get her in the water.'

"He thought I'd lost my mind, but he did what I asked him. In seven days I steamed up the Monongahela as fast as I could and made a fortune. You can imagine what Ralph said when he came along a couple of weeks later and found out I'd been there first."

Captain Bill tapped the wall where he was sitting. His blue eyes twinkled. "This was his boat, the *Goldenrod,* the biggest showboat ever built on the Mississippi. I bought it from him when he gave up the river."

There was the noise of a motor in the distance. A small helicopter appeared and swooped low over the water.

"Showboat people were always trying to think of something new to draw a crowd," said Brother Harry. "Sometimes they'd have a trained bear or maybe a lion. Or they'd take the showboat band to the telephone exchange in a little town and give the lady operator some tickets for the show. She'd plug in every subscriber she had and the band'd play a half-hour concert. But Bill had 'em all beat. He hired an airplane."

Captain Bill chuckled. "It was back in 1914, just before the First World War when a plane and a stunt pilot were a real novelty. I remembered one old farmer looking on as the pilot tuned up the engine.

'It ain't a-going to fly,' he told me.

"A minute later the plane climbed a couple of hundred feet.

'Ain't a-going to fly very high,' the farmer grumbled.

"Just then the plane sailed way up into the sky and disappeared in the clouds.

"The farmer watched and spit a big wad of tobacco. 'Well, anyway it can't carry no freight,' he said."

I went with Bill and Harry for a stroll about the boat to see any changes since my last visit. The show had been prospering and the paint on the walls of the theater that was the boat's reason for being, and the snowy Alps pictured on the curtain, seemed brighter. On the deck above was a battered calliope that for so long had been the symbol of the showboat, its metal tubes now red with rust. I had often heard from showboatmen of the special art of calliope-playing. A man might be a Paderewski on the piano and be a dismal failure at the calliope. Because of the steam pressure the instrument required enormous strength in the fingers; the player as well as being a musician had to be as powerful as a blacksmith. The best players ever on the river, I had heard, were Crazy Frank and a girl called Louisville Lou. When they took their places at the steamy keys they could be heard eight miles away.

"If you didn't have to put cotton in your ears it wasn't a good calliope," said Brother Harry.

Captain Bill nodded agreement. "Queer thing happened once with a calliope. We were playing for a couple of weeks in a town on the Bayou Teche, not far from New Orleans. A woman was in jail there waiting to be hanged—the only woman, so I heard, ever to be sentenced to execution in Louisiana. Every afternoon we played the calliope, and the second afternoon the condemned woman sent word to me how much she enjoyed the playing, and please would I have the calliope play something while she was being hung. I did what she asked, and we played *Nearer, My God, to Thee.* Human beings are hard to figure."

As we walked about the talk turned to the programs of the earlier days. Sometimes the show would be a popular melodrama; more often it would be a ministrel show or vaudeville and variety. A group of gay-clad chorus girls would appear, followed perhaps by a juggler or a Swiss bell-ringer. After this a local Houdini might emerge handcuffed from a water barrel or The Monkey-shines would shout commands at their trained baboons, racing madly on roller skates. These would be followed by Pat and Mike or Hans und Fritz in a riotous dialect routine, and perhaps a short comedy, *Why Men Leave Home.* A brief intermission would then occur with the Oleo, where members of the cast, doubling from some earlier appearance, would perform some specialty act, a black-faced tap dance or a sentimental song.

Then the regular show would proceed once more, with a magician who produced a pigeon out of a child's pocket, followed perhaps by an artist who made portraits of the Presidents out of different-colored dishrags, or an athletic young woman wearing white tights who posed as famous statues of ancient Greece and Rome. After this long preparation would come the headline act of the show, *Creation,* where a pretty girl swung on a great steel arm out over the audience and appeared to emerge from a budding flower; or *Fearnot,* who climbed a ladder to the top of the stage and dived into a tank of flaming oil. A moment later all the cast would join in the Grand Finale, followed in later days by a film travelogue such as *The Johnstown Flood.* The audience would go up the bank and drive off in their lantern-lit wagons, to talk about the thrilling events of the night until the next year.

It was almost dark and time for dinner now. We sat down

with the cast at the long table that almost filled the little dining room. They were a jolly crew, mostly battle-scarred veterans of carnivals and tent shows who for many years had shared Captain Bill's tribulations and triumphs.

Captain Bill ate heartily of the pot roast on his plate and chuckled again. "Showboat business was like show business everywhere. Plenty of times you went hungry. We were lucky, though. We had Mike, our pet rooster. He was a beautiful creature, a big Rhode Island Red, a combination prizefighter and Casanova. When food got low we'd land at some little country town and let Mike go hunting. He'd pick a fight with a local rooster, give him a good licking, and then come strutting up the gangplank, followed by the other rooster's harem. You can imagine what happened to those hens."

"Had another pet," remarked Brother Harry. "A pig we were awfully fond of, but he got so big we decided we couldn't keep him any longer and sold him to a Missouri farmer. We were in the middle of playing *Way Down East* that night when our pig comes squealing down the bank with a big piece of rope hanging from his neck. The farm where he'd been taken was seven miles back in the country but he'd heard the calliope and broke away. I guess that Missouri farmer's looking for him yet."

"Every showboat had a dog, too," added a stately, graying figure resembling Edwin Booth at one end of the table. "You

could always tell a dog off a showboat. He buried his bones a lot deeper than other dogs, getting ready for the hard times that were sure to be coming."

They talked of how the showboats followed the seasonal moods of the river—and the crops. In the spring they would go to the Monongahela and the coal mines; in the summer they would voyage down the Ohio and up the Mississippi, following the harvests of wheat and corn. In the fall they would start for the South where the owners of the plantations were preparing to pick and gin their cotton; in the winter they would roam the Louisiana bayous to lure the workers in the rice mills and the fields of sugarcane. They told of the parades, a feature of the older showboat life which was the delight of every dweller along the Mississippi. With his cast and crew, Captain Bill sometimes employed as many as sixty people. When they paraded through a town in their rainbow uniforms, he strung out the marchers so expertly that with the help of a dozen local boys properly costumed for the occasion the procession appeared to number at least two hundred. Now and then when some notable in a settlement died, Captain Bill would tactfully lend the showboat band to join in the funeral.

"Talking about funerals," said Edwin Booth. "I worked on a boat where the captain used to hire a hearse from the town undertaker when we paraded, with a big coffin inside all covered with flowers and half a dozen pallbearers marching behind. On top of the hearse there was a big sign: HE DIED LAUGHING AT THE SHOWBOAT."

The lively conversation continued. They talked of the tricks showboat captains used to elude the sheriff when there was no money to pay the license fee and the other grave crises that were constantly arising: how a grafting official of some little settlement would threaten to close the show unless a generous bribe was forthcoming by curtain time; or how the leading man would get hopelessly drunk and be unable to appear on the stage. The captain would introduce a telephone into the script and the lines of the missing hero would be read over the wire by an actor hidden in the wings. They told how when business reached the point of disaster a captain might temporarily abandon showboating and turn the vessel into a freight boat. The stage would be crowded with brooms and boxes of groceries; the seats would be occupied by sacks of potatoes, like dull-witted humans refusing to applaud. They told how one bitter winter Captain Bill's boat was frozen solid in the middle of the river. Too poor to buy coal for the stove in the cabin they burned some rubber tires they found abandoned on the bank, only to discover that the odor of the burning rubber was worse than the cold.

"That smell pretty near killed us," declared Bill's brother Ben sitting near me. "Our engineer said for ten years after he couldn't stand rubber anywhere around him. He'd take every rubber eraser out of his pencils and even pull the rubber threads out of his suspenders."

"A showboat captain had to be on his toes every minute or he'd have 'em cut off," said Captain Bill. "He had to be a pilot, a doctor, a priest, and a diver. He had to figure whether it was the time for a family of Swiss yodelers or whether it'd be better to have ladies dressed like butterflies swinging from wires by their teeth. Or maybe it'd be best to have a couple of fellows that played the Grand March from *Aida* on bicycle pumps. You never could tell what was going to happen, good or bad. One time business was terrible and we didn't know where our next meal was coming from, when we stopped at a big plantation down in Mississippi had a couple of thousand people working on it, white and black. The owner was feeling good and paid for the whole two thousand to come and see the show."

"Another time when we were starving we stopped at Gold Dust, Tennessee," put in the tall, Machiavellian figure opposite me, the villain in the *Goldenrod's* productions. "That's a tiny place a little way above Memphis. It'd been raining for days and the only way to get to the boat was to walk a couple of hundred yards through mud that came up to your knees. We figured we wouldn't even have a show that night, we were so sure nobody would come. But a couple of hours before curtain time the bank was packed with men and women, all country people from miles around. They hadn't seen a show for years and weren't going to miss one now. They all took off their shoes and stockings and waded through the mud and packed the boat to the railing."

Night had fallen now. Through the window I watched the lights of the Eads Bridge shimmering on the glassy water. The sudden blinding glare of a great searchlight on a towboat made me turn away. The boat groped its way toward the shore, the dazzling circle of light like the single eye of a Cyclops searching for his prey.

We went below to Captain Bill's office. It was nearing the time for the show and automobiles were assembling on the wharf, the drivers cursing occasionally as they struck one of the giant mooring rings set years before in the slippery cobblestones for the all-important steamboats.

There was a knock on the door soon after and a sad-eyed young man, whose frayed shirt and collar and shiny coat and trousers showed the scars of too many laundries and too many hot irons, entered and came timidly up to Captain Bill. "You don't need no chalk-drawer, do you, Captain? I can draw a picture of the Capitol in Washington in red, white, and blue chalk or Niagara Falls or a Mexican bullfight, all of 'em upside down."

Captain Bill shook his head regretfully. "Sorry, brother. Better go up and see the cook. He'll fix up a supper for you."

We walked through the theater and went backstage, noisy with the shifting of scenery. A new play was opening this particular night and the members of the cast were busy with a last-minute rehearsal of their parts. Standing in the wings were a dignified white-haired old man, wrinkled like an Egyptian papyrus, and a sweet-faced woman of similar age, obviously his wife. Both had been showboat actors, often on Captain Bill's boats, since childhood; now retired, they had come to visit Captain Bill and his company and relive their former days on the river. Beside them was a figure I saw whenever I came to the showboat, an old man with face reddened by long exposure to weather and alcohol, who had been engineer on the towboat which had moved Captain Bill and his company from place to place in their watery journeying. Long ago I had discovered that the *Goldenrod* was an informal non dues-paying club of which any ex-showboatman was a member.

The rehearsal ended. The cast went off to their dressing rooms for a quick change of costume.

I took advantage of the break to have a chat with the visitors.

"Worst time I ever had on a showboat was when Captain Bill went to Mobile over in Alabama," said the white-haired patriarch as we moved aside to avoid the canvas street of a New England village charging toward us. "A showboat captain'd try anything once, and when somebody told Bill all the people on the rivers in Alabama were millionaires he decided to make the trip. To get to Mobile the boat had to travel a long way in the Gulf of Mexico and riverboats weren't built for the ocean. Four times we started and had to turn back. The fifth time the pilot said the Gulf'd be smooth as asphalt, but we'd only been out a few minutes when a terrible storm came up with waves big as mountains. The boat began to leak in half a dozen places; it looked as if we were going to sink any minute. We all gathered on the stage and fell to our knees and began to pray."

He interrupted his speech as a village church dropped suddenly behind him, and went on. "Lord or somebody got us to Mobile, I don't know how. But when we arrived it was worse than the Gulf. The cotton crop was a failure that year and the rich farmers Bill'd heard about didn't have turnip greens and corn bread, much less fifty cents to pay for a showboat."

"It was terrible," said Captain Bill who had come over from supervising the scene-shifting for a moment. "Even the chickens and the turkeys were so skinny you felt too sorry for 'em to eat 'em. One night we gave a benefit performance for the poor people of Selma, Alabama. We should have given the benefit for ourselves. We were poorer than anybody there."

"Worst time I ever had was on a wild-animal boat," said the red-faced man. "Nothing but lions and tigers. The show went broke and the captain owned the steamboat it was traveling on had to take it over. He didn't know anything about handling a show, specially a show with wild animals, and pretty soon he was going broke too, without any money to feed 'em. You could hear that boat coming a hour before you could see her smokestacks. It wasn't the sound of her calliope, either. It was the roaring from the hungry lions and tigers. As long as that show was going around there was an awful lot of dogs and cats missing along the river."

It was time for the curtain to rise. I left the stage with Captain Bill and the others and took a seat at the back of the theater. It was a pleasant night to be on the water and almost every seat was occupied. But it was a different audience from the overalled men and sunbonneted women who would have attended fifty years before. These were city-dwellers, middle-aged individuals tired of motion pictures and hungry for any kind of living theater, or sophisticated young men and women come to hiss the villain and cheer the hero.

A tiny orchestra whose members later doubled as actors in the play took places before the stage and struck up a lively overture. The curtain rose jerkily and the show was on. The play

was drawn from the rich showboat repertory, a copy of *The Old Homestead*. I forgot its name half an hour after I'd left the boat. But it didn't really matter. The ideas behind the plots of showboat plays were always the same; they were always heartbreaking or terrifying accounts of suffering and villainy, at the last moment transformed by some unexpected event from tragedy to glory.

As the curtain rose the silvery-haired mother sitting before the glowing fireplace was telling her beautiful daughter the dreadful truth. the precious home in which the family had lived for five happy generations was soon to be lost forever. That morning she had learned how their erring husband and father, before committing suicide as a hopeless gambler, had tossed away the money to pay off the mortgage on a fatal turn of the cards. The bank was preparing to foreclose tomorrow. Gloating, the black-mustached villain entered and told the weeping mother he would supply the needed funds and save the beloved homestead; but only on condition the daughter would become his wife.

In cruel episode after episode the villain drew his evil web tighter. As the curtain rolled up for the final scene a score of gay-clad guests were assembled in the simple village church for the fateful wedding. The preacher, in the clutches of the villain as well because of a grievous error in his past, had solemnly read most of the marriage ceremony, and the villain was about to slip the ring onto the daughter's trembling finger, when a loud shout, "Stop!" resounded through the theater. A young man raced down the aisle, and climbing onto the stage, took the white-veiled heroine into his arms. It was her long-lost lover, a sailor believed to have perished at sea, now a rich man with a fortune made in Australia. Soon the wedding bells rang out, but not for the groom originally intended. The returned lover marched triumphantly down the aisle with the smiling bride on his arm; while the thwarted villain stood watching in the wings, too dazed even to utter his curses. The audience laughed and hissed him noisily.

"Years ago they'd have really meant the hissing," said Captain Bill. "This was a slice of real life to 'em. Once up the Mononga-hela when we were playing *Uncle Tom's Cabin,* a coal miner jumped onto the stage with a pistol and told Simon Legree if he didn't stop horsewhipping Uncle Tom he'd pay for it with his life."

The audience filed out slowly. The wharf blazed with light as the drivers of the tight-packed cars started their motors. The lights went out as the cars sped away. The wharf grew quiet, deserted.

I went with Captain Bill to his office for a good-night beer. A towboat moved slowly past the window, on its asthmatic way upstream. The pilot blew his whistle and blinked his lights in salute. Captain Bill smiled and clicked the lights in the office.

There was a new knock on the door. A member of the audience I had noticed lingering on the deck entered, a middle-aged man wearing a shabby, once-blue sport coat and threadbare red trousers. "You don't need no magic act, do you, Captain Bill? I been playing all the big shows in New York, B. F. Keith's Palace and all of 'em. I can hypnotize a dog in ten seconds, a boy in a minute, and a full-grown man in two. I can cut off a woman's head with a guillotine or saw her in half. How about it, Captain Bill?"

The towboat blew a melancholy whistle as in answer.

CHAPTER

7

CUMBERLAND
JOURNEY

"Flitter Jim's the finest-educated man around here," said the grizzled mountaineer standing on his rickety porch. "He can read and write and tell time by the clock. You learn plenty in that Frankfort Penitentiary."

I was walking along a rocky creek, one of the headwaters of the beautiful Cumberland River which flowed into the hill-bordered Ohio, then into the muddy Mississippi, and at last into the sea. It was many years ago, when this Cumberland Valley was almost as remote as China, surrounded by great mountain walls and unbroken by the roads which spread everywhere in the low-lands; the only way to travel was on foot or horseback along the stony watercourses where I was now making my laborious way.

I had known the mountaineers a long time, ever since my Kentucky childhood; I had known them when as a young man

I had often wandered across these pine-covered ridges; I had known them also on the Mississippi, after they had come to Louisville and Cincinnati and Memphis to find work lacking in the settlements near their barren farms; unfit for the grim demands of a mechanical age, they had built shantyboats of boards they found along the banks of some river town and drifted down toward New Orleans. Others more ambitious had become towboat deckhands or mates or now and then a steamboat pilot.

For several weeks I had been seeing them once more in their native hills, talking to their wives, who if the need arose, could take the dust-covered spinning wheel standing off in the shadows and make their clothing from the wool of the sheep grazing in the green valleys. I had slept in cabins so primitive there was no lamp or even a candle, only a torch made from pitch pine.

The weather forecast I had heard on the radio in Pineville was discouraging: a wide-spreading storm was moving up from the Gulf of Mexico. But my time was growing short and there were still a few things I wanted to investigate of that mountain culture which had so much affected the speech and customs of the river-dwellers below. I decided to throw caution to the winds and take my chances. I had no inkling how my travels here were soon to show in a dramatic climax how close was the link between this little stream where I was walking and the mighty Mississippi hundreds of miles away.

I asked my grizzled informant on the porch of the cabin where I had halted how far it was to the home of Flitter Jim where I had been told I could spend the night.

" 'Tain't far at all, brother," he answered. "Ain't more'n a mile."

All morning I plodded along the creek, sometimes wading through ankle-deep pools, sometimes leaving it to take a path alongside that led up a steep mountain. Swiftly its waters ran, now coursing in foamy waves over jagged stones, now almost lost under a mass of tangled logs caught on the barbed-wire fence of a farm. Toward noon, exhausted and footsore, I saw a log cabin

126

where an old man was working in a tiny garden. I asked how far it was now to Flitter Jim's.

"Ain't much more than a mile," he answered. "Come in and set awhile."

I accepted his invitation gladly and followed him into his cabin.

He examined me critically. "You look all wore out. I'll git you something to eat."

Soon I was sitting at a long table before a plate filled with steaming pork and turnip greens. Off in the corner I noticed a skinny dog with a woebegone expression that told beyond doubt he was being punished for some serious crime. I asked my host how he had offended.

The old man's face hardened. He pointed to a widening of the creek in front of the cabin. "Ain't ever been but one real fish in that creek, a big catfish weighing twenty pounds. I been trying for years to catch him and never could. Ever since that dog's been a puppy he's liked to catch fish and frogs and anything in the water. Last night he was sitting on the bank and that big catfish come along and he reached in and got him just like he'd throwed a line. I sure ain't going to have no dog around that's a better fisherman than me."

He urged me to try some of the innumerable varieties of pickles, the pride of mountain housewives, scattered around the table. "My old woman's best pickle-maker in Clay County. She's away helping my daughter have her first baby."

He jumped up suddenly from the table and brushed something from my jacket. "It's a measuring worm going down you. If he measured you all the way to your shoes he'd be measuring you for your coffin."

Through the window I saw a lean figure coming down the creek. He knocked at the door, and at a word from my host entered and took a seat at the table. He was a sad-faced man and spoke little; he gulped down the contents of his plate as though he had not tasted food for several days. He was still eating when

I started to take my leave. He arose hurriedly and showed me some celluloid rings of different colors.

"You wouldn't want no ring, would you, brother?" he asked. "I learned how to make 'em out of old combs in the Walls, that's the penitentiary. If you got a old comb to give me a ring's fifteen cents. If I give you a comb it'll cost you a quarter."

I continued along the creek. All afternoon I trudged on wearily, hearing always from each lanky mountaineer I passed that Flitter Jim's cabin was only a mile away. It was nearing sunset when the house came into view, an impressive dwelling made of hand-hewn pine boards instead of the usual logs.

Flitter Jim welcomed me warmly, a huge bald-headed man with a curious choking laugh somewhat resembling the sizzling of a teakettle. I washed in the tin basin on the porch, followed in my ablutions by a stocky little salesman for a hardware company and a fat man selling cattle feed. Flitter Jim's generous hospitality—unpaid like all native to the area—was famous throughout the mountains.

To reach the house I had been compelled to cross an inlet by means of a footlog common to the region. Flitter Jim showed me how, by adjusting it a certain way, it would turn and throw any unwary visitor into the water.

"If somebody I don't like comes around I fix it so it turns thataway," he remarked with a wink. "Don't hurt 'em none but they don't generally come back."

We went inside. Flitter Jim's wife, a thin, sunbonneted woman, appeared and began preparing supper.

I accompanied Flitter Jim as he went to milk the cow mooing mournfuly at the wooden fence surrounding the house. Blue jays and scarlet-capped Kentucky cardinals flew about in the pines overhead, chirping drowsily as they prepared for the coming of night. Beyond us the mountains stretched smoky ridge after ridge to the darkening horizon.

The milking was quickly ended. We returned to the house to find supper ready, and sat down at the hand-hewn table.

According to the mountain custom Flitter Jim's quiet wife did not join us. The Cumberland women served the men first, then ate afterward.

Flitter Jim and the other two men leaned back in their chairs when they had finished the meal and began to chew huge wads of tobacco.

"Hear you're trying to get a post office here in the creek," said the little hardware salesman, whose long black hair gave him the appearance of an Indian.

"That's right," agreed Flitter Jim. "Trouble is we ain't got enough business." He chewed his cud meditatively. "What we need's a fellow like Uncle Ace Combs over at Pine Mountain."

"Heard about him. Got a post office there all by himself, didn't he?"

Flitter Jim nodded. "That's right. Ace'd been trying to get it for twenty years but government people kept telling him wasn't enough people around there to buy a sheet of stamps a year. They said even if the people wanted to send letters they couldn't 'cause they couldn't read or write. But Ace fixed things mighty smart. First he asked everybody to send for them big mail-order catalogues—them catalogues weighs plenty and he figured that'd make plenty of business—and then when the people said they couldn't do the writing to ask, he wrote the letters for 'em. And then he told 'em to send off for the newspapers in Louisville and Lexington and when they said they couldn't read he said he'd read the papers to 'em."

"Them newspapers is plenty heavy too," put in the feed man.

"That's right. Then he said it was wrong for 'em not to know nothing about their kinfolk that'd gone to work in St. Louis and Detroit and them places. So he wrote the letters for 'em and read the answers that come back. And then when the government people said, 'All right, you got enough business now to open the post office, but who's going to carry the mail?' Ace says, 'I will.' He was seventy if he was a day but I seen him a couple of times, riding on his horse with a couple of mail sacks, proud as a turkey

cock just drove off a hawk. I figure if we don't get a post office here pretty quick I'll get rid of my old woman and put my picture in one of them Lonely Hearts magazines, and then all them pretty girls'll write so many letters wanting to marry me we'll have the biggest post office in the State of Kentucky."

It was nearing election time and the talk shifted to politics. I glanced at the campaign advertisements in the little weekly newspaper from nearby Manchester as it was passed around the table. A candidate for county clerk promised a dog for every man in the mountains. A candidate for sheriff proclaimed that he had been married for thirty-five years and never had any trouble with his wife and children—he added that if he was elected it would be the same with the people of Clay County. A candidate for the crucially important office of jailer declared that anyone arrested, while in his jail could be assured of having the same food the jailer had on his own table.

A young woman wearing a faded housedress, who lived in the nearby cabin, came in to bring our hostess some preserves and went off with her into the kitchen. I learned that she was the great-granddaughter of a famous feudist in the region. The feuds which had once been the scourge of the hills were revived occasionally but on a much milder scale; now they were delicately known as "family trouble."

"Had plenty of family trouble here just a while ago," said

Flitter Jim. "Big Tom Mothers killed Little Slick Bates in a argument and wasn't no preacher around so the family buried Little Slick and figured they'd have the funeral in the spring. Funeralizing we calls it here when you have to wait thataway. Spring come and they got everything ready for Slick, and then they found out wasn't nobody around could read the lines of the hymns right except Big Tom who'd killed him. Course they didn't want to do it, but somebody had to read the lines or there couldn't be no funeral. So they got Tom. Things was going fine and Little Slick's family and Tom's family and everybody was crying way they ought to, when Slick's father decided Big Tom was reading the lines kind of sarcastic, and they started arguing. And pretty soon somebody, I don't know who, fired a shot. And in a couple of minutes they was blazing away like that book I read once about the battle of Waterloo. Lucky wasn't nobody hurt. But ain't no preacher that'll come here since."

To my surprise I discovered that despite his seeming sophistication, Flitter Jim, like most Cumberland-dwellers, was deeply religious, a profound believer in the tenets of the Scotch Covenanters who had settled the country a hundred and fifty years before. To him the ways of modern religion were as evil as the worship of the Golden Calf.

"Better have a little hymn-singing before we go to bed," he declared.

He picked up a worn songbook and in a high-pitched voice led us in some mountain hymns. His face as he ended was radiant, then quickly grew solemn.

"They're a-talking about starting a Sunday school over at the Elk Fork church," he declared. "But ain't a word about a Sunday school in the Bible. If they start that Sunday school wouldn't surprise me noway if Lord don't send a bolt of lightning and burn the church down."

He restored the book to its place.

The two drummers and I were about to retire to the adjoining room where beyond the door I could see four single beds, when a sudden tiny shadow swept past me from somewhere up near the ceiling and I heard the faint whirring of tiny wings. An instant later a little screech owl struck at a hole in the corner.

Flitter Jim glanced at the little bird with pride. "Some people likes blacksnakes. But a blacksnake ain't nothing to a screech owl for catching mice."

I set out again in the morning. On the way I met a serious-looking individual riding a horse with a black bag strapped behind the saddle. He rode alongside me for a little while; I discovered he was a local doctor on his way to nearby Manchester to buy some needed drugs. Something in his manner struck me as different from that of the usual country physician; I asked where he had studied medicine.

He glanced at me oddly. "They made me a male nurse when I was sent to the penitentiary," he said.

It had seemed extraordinary when I first came to these hills that so many mountaineers, obviously not criminal types, had served terms in prison. And then I learned the reason. It arose from the mountaineer's fierce spirit of independence which was

the foundation of his character, on which all his actions depended. Most of the prison sentences were for making moonshine; corn was the only crop he could plant on the rocky slopes that were his farmland. Without highways or railroads he could not send the corn to compete with the crops of the abundant lowlands. The only way he could ship his harvest was to turn it into liquid freight—whisky. It was his corn, he argued to himself; thus it was his liquor, his legal property, with the inalienable right to sell it as he pleased. Anyone such as a revenue officer who interfered was acting in an illegal fashion. It was as lawful to shoot the revenuer as to shoot a man trying to steal his timber or his cow. In such a case no disgrace was attached to prison; it was the law that was at fault, not the moonshiner.

Shortly after noon I arrived at Manchester, county seat of Clay County, one of the goals of my mountain journey. The little town, which had known much violence in its past but was now settling down to a peaceful existence, was famous for its local judge known as Judge Honey, a nickname bestowed because of his unique court procedure. Every person who appeared before him for sentencing, man, woman, or juvenile delinquent, he addressed as Honey; his favorite concluding line, heard by many a saddened offender, was: "Honey, I hate to do this to you but I have to give you sixty days, Honey."

I attended his court; at his invitation I sat beside him on the worn bench. The Manchester police force, like the crew of the *Nancy Brig*, consisted of a single officer who acted as chief of police, chief of detectives, and the entire uniformed department. The police force brought forward a nervous little blond man, from his manner and actions obviously a stranger to the region.

Judge Honey studied the prisoner. "What you been doing, Honey?"

The stranger wiped his sweating face. "Had some liquor on me I bought in Louisville, Judge. I'm sure sorry."

The police force produced a pint flask of bonded whisky.

The Judge leaned forward in his chair. "Was the top broke open?"

The police force examined the cork intently. "No, Judge. But it was fixing to be broke."

Judge Honey shook his head. "Fixing to be broke ain't broken." He turned to the prisoner again. "Let me see your hands, Honey."

The other obeyed in wonder.

The Judge examined the toil-callused palms. "You're a hard-working man all right, Honey." He turned to the police force. "Case dismissed. Let him go."

A stout country woman from far back in the hills bustled into the room, breathless from climbing the stairs. "My sister Goldie ain't coming in today with her boy got arrested way you told her to, Judge," she panted. "She was going to get a tooth pulled the same time, and when she looked at the almanac she seen this week the zodiac signs is in the head and it'd bleed mighty bad. She says she'll come in next week when the signs is in the back."

Circuit Court, a degree higher, was in session in the County Courthouse not far away. I walked over for a visit. The town square was crowded with mud-spattered horses and automobiles; paved roads around Manchester in those days were an almost unknown luxury. I climbed the steps of the Courthouse. Its windows were blackened with soot, the paint on the sashes peeled away from long exposure to the mountain winters. I went inside to the smoky courtroom.

The Judge, a solemn figure befitting the office, was selecting the Grand Jury. He turned to the tobacco-munching farmers arranged before him on a double row of chairs. "Before I swear you in is there anybody sitting here that's under indictment? I don't want nobody on my Grand Jury that's under indictment."

The selection of the jury ended and the trials already prepared began. The Judge called the name of a defendant. The accused man failed to appear; in ordinary procedure beyond the hills his bond would have been instantly forfeited. But not by the code of the mountains.

"He's getting in his corn, Judge," a clerk explained. "His wife's been mighty sick and today's first chance he's had to get to it."

The Judge postponed the case until the crop was harvested.

The trials ended. The Judge led me into his little office behind the courtroom. We were joined by two of the town's leading lawyers, keen-witted men reminiscent of the old Yankee horse-traders, possessed of a dry, cynical sense of humor.

The Judge left the room for a moment.

"Too bad you wasn't here when old Judge Lew Lewis used to be around," said one of the lawyers, a portly figure with hair so glossy it shone like a mirror, as he aimed with startling accuracy at a distant cuspidor. "He was a real card. Told his Grand Jury, if you see a fellow going down the creek leading a hound dog and carrying a banjo or guitar, indict him. 'Cause if he ain't done nothing yet he sure is going to."

"What about Judge Lew and that tough fellow named Big Harm over in Leslie County?" remarked the other lawyer, a young man with the shrewd, quizzical face of one much older. "Big Harm said he was going to kill three of the top fellows over in Hyden. Judge Lew didn't want any of 'em hurt and he knew the sheriffs couldn't handle Big Harm when he got drunk and started shooting. So instead of trying to hold down Big Harm he put the three others under a peace bond to keep out of his way."

"Another time they was having a big baptizing in the creek," said the lawyer with the glossy hair. "Judge Lew went to it with all the prisoners in the jail that wanted to be saved. When they came out of the water he congratulated 'em with one hand and pointed the pistol he was holding in the other."

The Judge returned, his solemnity gone now that the day's work was over. He glanced at the older attorney a moment. "Be careful of Stringy Bob sitting there next to you," he said to me dryly. "When he takes a case he's got two prices. Always asks people that come to him if they want a case with or without witnesses."

The young lawyer nodded. "Hope what happened to Hard-shell Luke Estill ain't going to happen to Bob. Hardshell was the biggest lawyer around here till he lost both his witnesses. One of 'em died and the other moved away."

I left soon after and went into a bleak room a few doors away for a visit with the sheriff. I was studying the weird faces of the men wanted for various crimes glaring from the handbills pinned to the walls, when a mountaineer from a distant hollow came in to inquire about some property up for auction. The visitor was on his way out the door when the sheriff called him back. "Mace, I just heard that Will Scoggins shot a fellow up Red Bird Creek this morning. Stop in at his cabin on your way back home and tell him I want him to come here tomorrow, will you? And tell him to bring some clothes with him, 'cause he's got to stay in jail for a while."

A procession of overalled mountaineers followed: a father worried about his son who had been arrested in Memphis, an old man come to complain about a neighbor whose hog was constantly breaking through a fence and spoiling his garden.

A gentle-mannered individual I knew to be a noted ex-sheriff entered. His voice and appearance gave him the air of a kindly preacher instead of a man who had captured some of the most desperate killers in the hills.

"Never used a handcuff all my life," he told me. "And never once had a fellow that ran off. A man here they called Easy Joe killed somebody and the Judge sentenced him to Frankfort Pen for life. I had five other prisoners to go down the same time with him and if I took 'em all they'd have packed my car mighty tight. Easy Joe stood there looking a minute. 'Sheriff, I sure hate to crowd you,' he said. 'My brother's driving down to Frankfort today to buy a plow. How about my going along with him to the Walls?'

'All right, Joe,' I answered. 'You go on down with him. If you get there before I do, just wait till I come.'

"His brother's car was faster than mine. When I got there he was standing out in front of the gate."

He smiled in reminiscence. "Had another murderer just like him once. A fellow we nicknamed Possum Tom. Judge gave him life, like the other. I was taking him to the Pen on the train and we had to change trains at Corbin. I left him on the platform

so I could buy the tickets. 'You wait right here, Possum,' I told him. 'I figure I'll be gone just about five minutes.' But there were a lot of people at the ticket window and there was some kind of mix-up, so it was over half an hour before I was through. When I got out to the platform again I saw Possum pacing up and down, looking terrible nervous.

'Golly, where you been all this time, Sheriff?' he said when he saw me. 'I was getting mighty worried you wasn't coming back.' "

It was dark now and I saw a light in the barred building behind the Courthouse that I knew was the County Jail. I knocked loudly on the iron gate. As I waited for someone to open I could see shadowy figures upstairs moving behind a grating; I could hear a harmonica playing gaily. A moment later the jailer appeared, a towering Western-looking figure known as Cowboy, who had campaigned for his office on horseback, dressed in full cattle-punching regalia.

He accompanied me into his gray-walled office. Upstairs there came always the sound of tapping feet, following the rhythmic beat of the musician.

"I treat 'em right and they treat me right," said Cowboy. "This jail's so old you can cut your way out quicker than a raccoon chews through a egg crate, and about a year back a fellow they called Black Jack sawed some bars and ran away. I went down to the creek where his family was living. 'It ain't right the way Black Jack did me, Ace,' I told his brother. 'I gave him plenty of privileges and now he's run off like that it's going to hurt my reputation bad.'

"The brother didn't answer for a minute. 'Guess he didn't think nothing about that, Cowboy,' he said. 'I'm going out in the woods where he's hiding and tell him right away.'

"When I got up next morning Black Jack's sitting on the jail steps. He was mighty sorry."

In the barred room upstairs the merry playing of the harmonica grew louder.

Cowboy listened with approval. "Like to hear a harmonica or a fiddle going," he declared. "Never had trouble yet with a fellow that plays music."

He went out in the street to buy some tobacco.

A grizzled prisoner who had come in with a pile of dishes gazed after him with affection. "I been in jails all over," he told me. "From New Orleans to Chicago. You can't beat Cowboy nowhere for running a jail."

I ate a quick supper in a little café where a jukebox droned out doleful mountain ballads, and hearing of a Holiness meeting, hurried over. It was a tiny church, hardly much larger than a country store. But the little congregation of shabbily clad men and women made up in energy and devotion what they lacked in numbers. For half an hour they laughed and wept, sang and shouted, leaped and danced. At last, physically weary and emotionally spent, they grew quiet.

The preacher began to talk in a low voice. "People wants to know why us Holiness Folks gits like this," he told his listeners. "Why we git so happy singing and dancing. I'll tell you how it is. It's thisaway.

"The other day I seen a fellow holding a string up in the air. 'What you holding that string for, brother?' I asked him.

'I'm a flying a kite,' he said.

'I can't see no kite, brother,' I answered. 'Can you see the kite?'

'No, brother, I can't see it,' he told me. 'It's too high up in the air for me to see it. But I can sure feel it tugging.' That's the way it is with Holiness Church."

In the morning the sky was ominous, with inky black clouds sweeping across the horizon. I went on nevertheless, up one remote creek after another. For several days I continued, the predicted storm ever threatening but failing to arrive. Always I met the same stern-appearing but always kindly men and women. In the mountains the stranger was sacred as the guest in the tent of an Arab nomad; I heard legends how in the old days a feud battle had halted to let a stranger pass. Now and then I saw a gaunt mountaineer working busily to turn his harvest of logs into a great raft that would race down the creek when it would be swollen with the expected rain. Sometimes as a result of the watery voyage he would be fascinated by the life of the river. After selling his timber to a sawmill along the bank, he would build a shantyboat and float with the current, to join his mountain fellows turned shantyboater far down the Mississippi.

I stopped to rest late one afternoon in the cabin of a gentle old man known as Uncle John Fiddler. A gale had begun to blow and the air was chilly; my frail host urged me to sit close to the fire. He looked at the branches of the trees swaying violently outside and shivered.

"It's a cold wind blowing, brother," he said.

He sat silent for a while, his feeble hands almost touching the flaming wood, then with his spirit a little revived, turned toward me. "Want to hear some music, brother?"

"I don't know of a time when I didn't want to hear music."

"I'll play you some fiddle tunes."

He took down a cracked violin from the wall and began playing shakily. "Used to go around everywhere playing my fiddle. All over these here mountains. Once I went to Carolina and once I played for them Indian people down in the Great Smoky Mountains. When I finished them Indian people clapped so hard you couldn't have heard a gun fired."

His wrinkled wife was hobbling about the room, using an old gun handle as a crutch. She glanced at his trembling hands and his shaking head, then fixed her gaze on the violin angrily.

"It's that fiddle gives him them shakes," she said. "All his life it's been that way, fiddle, fiddle, fiddle. That there music ain't nothing but sin."

The gale outside heightened and began to whistle shrilly through the cracks in the log walls. The flaming pine wood in the fireplace flickered and began to burn out.

The old man's shivering increased. He put down the fiddle

and drawing close to the fire again, rubbed his hands feebly over the dying coals. "It's a cold wind blowing, brother," he said.

Soon after, I came in sight of the Pine Mountain Settlement School, established years before in the wilderness to bring book-learning to the education-hungry inhabitants.

A light rain had begun to fall as I arrived. The bright-eyed little girl who greeted me hurried off, in a moment returning with the head of the school, the reserved but kindly Miss Petit who had become a legend throughout the Cumberlands.

A fierce blast of wind shook the windows. Miss Petit looked troubled. "I just heard the forecast from Lexington. The weather's getting worse. When the creek comes up with a heavy rain we can be marooned here for weeks."

I sat next to her as we ate a Spartan supper of milk and corn bread, surrounded by scores of bright-eyed little girls like the one who had greeted me on my arrival.

"These mountain children are like their parents," she said. "They're incredibly anxious to learn. I waked up one morning a little while ago to find a sweet little girl standing on the porch with a paper scrawled by one of her neighbors pinned to her dress, explaining that she had been sent by her grandfather so she could learn to read and write. The note went on to say that the grandfather didn't have the few dollars we require for our token tuition, so instead he was leaving the chief product of his farm, which he hoped would pay the fee. We opened the big box the little girl had brought and found several gallons of moonshine whisky. We're a church-supported school, against any kind of liquor, and didn't know what to do. In the end we took the little girl and poured the tuition fee into the creek."

The children went off to bed and we moved to the living room. The wind had subsided but the rain was falling steadily. We sat talking before a crackling log.

"Odd things are always happening here," Miss Petit said. "I hurt my ankle riding horseback one afternoon and decided to stop in the nearest cabin. It was a simple log cabin like all the others, but standing in the middle I was amazed to see a beautiful piano. The old man living there with his wife and daughter told me how it got there. Years before, he'd sold a raft of logs at the mouth of one of the forks of the Cumberland and was trying to think what kind of present he'd get his little girl, when a piano salesman came along and suggested he buy his daughter a piano. The mountaineer thought it a fine idea, and the same day he put a piano on a little barge and started it up the river the way he'd come down with the raft. After terrible difficulties he got it to the foot of the mountains here, and then he and all his neighbors started pushing and rolling it across the ridges toward his cabin. Finally they reached his home and took it inside. And then they realized the awful truth. It was a beautiful piano. But there wasn't anybody in the mountains here who could play it. When I met him the father was past seventy; the little girl was now a grown woman with her own granddaughter.

'Lady, that piano's been a-setting there for thirty years and ain't nobody ever touched them keys,' the father told me wistfully. 'Lady, maybe you can play that piano.'

"Fortunately I could and I go back to the cabin every month to play for the family and all the neighbors. And their faces light up as if I were an angel with a harp I'd brought down from heaven."

I was wakened just after dawn by a faint knock and a childish voice at the door; looking out the window, I saw the rain falling in torrents. I hurried down to breakfast to find Miss Petit sitting nervously at the table awaiting my arrival.

"It's a cloudburst and the radio says it's the same all over the Mississippi Valley," she declared. "In a few hours the creek will be impassable. We'll get you a good horse and try to take you on a shortcut over the mountain on the road to Pineville. If you don't make it you'll have to come back and put up with all our funny ways for a month."

I gulped down some coffee and in a few moments, accom-

panied by a sturdy young mountaineer as guide, was on a horse riding through the deluge. For a short distance we rode along the creek, no longer the placid brook I had traveled the day before but rapidly becoming a rushing river, then started climbing a stony trail that wound up a steep mountain. The whole rocky slope as far as the eye could see was a series of miniature cataracts; the trail was a continuous muddy Niagara. Time after time our horses slipped and almost fell on the flooding stones; each time they recovered and struggled upward. The wind had risen again and was blowing a full gale now; the raincoat I had hopefully worn was useless. Soon I was drenched to the skin. With the wind the rain became blinding; I could only vaguely distinguish the shape of the rider ahead. Our horses seemed to be floundering across a raging yellow sea.

We reached the top of the mountain; the panting horses plunged onto the path downward. The wind lessened on this side of the mountain. But the blinding rain grew heavier. Often our horses slid down the rocks as though they had been greased for a toboggan slide. At last, with a sigh of relief I saw the hard-surfaced road to Pineville shining through the mist. We reached it soon after. I hailed a passing car and bidding my guide a grateful good-by, was quickly on my way.

"She's a bad one, brother," said the driver, a drummer on his way to introduce a new soft drink to the area. "Hear over the radio the Red Cross is getting ready to look after all the people moving out. Bet these creeks 'll rise thirty feet by night."

We drove to Pineville, busy little mountain metropolis, to find the streets coursing with water from the downpour. My Samaritan drove me to the railroad station.

"Don't know whether you can get through to Covington, brother," said the ticket agent. "Track's under water a big part of the way. We're sending a locomotive ahead of the train to see if we can make it."

I climbed aboard one of the waiting coaches. Along the riverbank we moved slowly, the locomotive a short distance before us feeling the way like a blind man unsure of his path, tapping with his cane. The steep slopes of the mountains hemming us in were like the sides of a funnel, pouring the torrential rain into the spout that was the river. At times going around a bend I could see that the wheels of the forward coaches were almost submerged in the rushing water. Often the train came to a stop as the locomotive ahead signaled us to wait while the men aboard explored the flooded tracks, then moved on slowly again after the signal it was safe to proceed. The river seemed to swell higher and higher by the moment as we descended toward the lowlands. By the time we reached the junction point of the railroad where the line branched away the river had become a raging yellow monster, sweeping away houses, bridges, and everything in its path. Buildings far up on the bank were surrounded, with muddy waves lapping at the windows.

The torrential rain showed no sign of slackening. When we reached the Ohio next day, out of the train window I could see the telltale signs I knew so well of a swiftly rising river. In the newspaper I bought from a train butcher I read that the rainfall was breaking records everywhere from the Appalachians in the East to the Rockies in the West. Streams big and little were overflowing their banks from Minneapolis and St. Paul in the North to New Orleans in the South, everywhere in the great Valley. Hundreds were already homeless; damage was already in the millions. In a few days the usually tranquil Ohio would be raging like its tributary, the Cumberland, I had just descended. The same swelling currents were pouring down the Illinois, the Missouri, the White, the Arkansas, the Sunflower, the Yazoo. Soon the Father of Waters, with the rains of half the entire country pouring into its narrow channels, like a furious animal escaping from its cage, would burst its bonds everywhere and devastate the countryside.

Though I did not know it then, riding my horse that morning up storm-swept Pine Mountain, I had witnessed the beginning of one of the great Mississippi floods.

CHAPTER

A TOUCH
OF
CHINA

The battered little fishing boat left Barataria Bay and drifted slowly toward the green wall of the Mississippi marshes stretching endlessly to the horizon.

"It's crazy, having Chinamen on the Mississippi," said the lanky fisherman who had brought me over from the sleepy little town of Lafitte, not far from New Orleans. "When you see 'em you'll figure you been drinking too much of that Cajun wine they call Twenty Percent."

As he spoke what at first sight seemed a curious-shaped island came into view, with shrimp boats and scores of craft of all varieties moored alongside.

"Fellows runs this place is named Wu and Sing," said my companion called Arkansas Ike, brushing back the dark hair streaming down over his face, reddened by whisky and weather.

"Some people says they're okay, but I don't trust no kind of China-man. Had a friend up in Helena where I come from played poker with a Chinaman once, and he said the Chinaman knowed every card he had the minute he picked 'em up, just like he was using a X ray."

The curious island with its encircling vessels came closer; our fishboat bumped against a piling. I climbed a makeshift ladder alongside and reached the top. Before me was a sight I had never expected to see in America, an enormous wooden platform several acres in extent, set high on stilts, and completely surrounded by water; on it everywhere were little groups of sheds and houses, with wooden footwalks in between, the exact counterpart of the fishermen's villages I had seen in Malaysia and Borneo. For many years I had heard rumors from steamboatmen of these Chinese shrimp platforms built somewhere at the mouth of the Mississippi and sought to find their location; but my search was always fruitless. No riverman, no government official I met had ever seen one or had any idea of their whereabouts. They were shrouded in as much mystery as the Lost Atlantis. Then I visited Lafitte where the Chinese owners came for supplies, and I met Arkansas Ike who stayed on the wooden islands often—and my search was ended.

"Here comes Chang," said Arkansas Ike, as a portly Chinese

walked slowly forward to meet us. "He runs the place when Mr. Wu and Mr. Sing ain't around."

The newcomer, a genial elderly man with a head as bald and shiny as a Chinese porcelain statue, greeted me cordially, and conducted me on a tour of the extraordinary settlement. It was like a quick voyage around the world; the languages I heard were numerous as those at the Tower of Babel. "You no catch shrimp today, Kin?" asked a tall Slav as he passed a little Filipino walking with a pretty wife and toddling baby. Drying a net was a Portuguese from West Africa, dark as ebony.

"We got plenty kinds people here," said Chang, in accents that were a bizarre combination of Cantonese and Cajun and the speech of the natives of rural America with whom he was chiefly associated. "Now not got many. Not right season swimp. Swimp next month, month after maybe. Yes? When swimp come bushels swimp, bushels people. Bring swimp to platform. All kinds people. Cajun people, American people—how you call him—hillbillies people, couple hundred people, maybe. Okay people. Plenty okay. Yes?"

He showed me the drying platforms that were the reason for the island's creation—long, narrow elevations built in waves, like a series of roller coasters. Here workers were taking shrimp from huge kettles of boiling brine and placing them at the top of the wooden hills so that any water would drain quickly away. For days the shrimp would lie in the sun, protected if it rained, by wide tarpaulins. When the last drop of moisture had vanished they would go off to the shelling machines nearby, revolving drums with long spikes inside, like medieval instruments of torture. There they would be shipped off to Chinese restaurants from New York to California.

"Chinese people different American people," explained Chang. "American people like swimp plenty water. Chinese people like 'em plenty dry, like paper. This why swimp platform come here, long time maybe. Yes? Some say first man Chinese fellow Canton, see plenty swimp Barataria Bay, build platform, tell

papa, grandpapa, brothers, cousins, Canton, 'Come Barataria. Fine swimp.' Other people say Filipino fellow name Kin Ting, say same thing Filipinos. Anyway, smart fellow, same as Chinese, know Chinese like dried swimp, know plenty Chinese restaurants New York, San Francisco. Build swimp platform. Die plenty rich man."

Soon after an old Filipino padded up to him and spoke a quiet word. Chang excused himself and hurried away.

My attention was distracted for a moment as a school of fish dashed frantically out of the water beside the wooden path where I was walking, trying to escape a small but voracious shark. Two sea gulls poised on nearby pilings darted suddenly down to join the chase.

Arkansas Ike's drawling voice brought me back to the platform. "Chang's told you plenty," he said. "What he ain't told you is the shrimp platforms is about the toughest places there is anywhere. They're like that French Foreign Legion I seen in a picture show up in Helena once. Fellow done some kind of bad crime somewheres and gets here he's safe as if he's a kid singing in a Baptist church on Sunday. Them Chinese'd let the detectives cut their tongues out before they'd tell on him. And he ain't said a word about smuggling. Guess you heard about that, didn't you?"

"I've heard rumors but I don't believe all I hear."

"Well, you can believe that, all right. Ain't a week goes by they don't get a boatful of Chinamen smuggled in from Cuba

149

or Mexico for $500 a head. Ain't but two weeks ago I heard there was twenty Chinamen coming in a boat to be smuggled in to work in Texas, when the Coast Guard seen 'em and started after 'em. But the smugglers had everything ready. They had the Chinese tied to a big heavy chain, so they just dropped the chain overboard and the Chinamen went along. When the Coast Guard come up to the boat wasn't anything left of them Chinamen except some marks on the side of the boat where the chain going over cut the wood."

He turned for confirmation to a blond little man whose overalls reeked of the shrimp he had been catching, and who had come from his cabin a few steps away to join in the conversation. "I'm telling it right, ain't I, Hoppin' John? You was here when it happened. You seen the FBI men that come in uniform and everything, didn't you?"

The other gave a grunt of disgust. "Don't you believe a word he says, Mister. He's been reading too many of them *True Horror* comic books. Besides, he's sore 'cause he tried to sell Chang some lousy shrimp and Chang was too smart to buy 'em. Some fellows did come in uniform all right. But they was electric men from New Orleans. They come to fix the light plant."

Arkansas Ike was not convinced. "What about them stories how everybody on the shrimp platforms all of a sudden went crazy about flowers and started growing 'em in pots all around their houses, and then the FBI come and found all the flowers was poppies. The Chinamen was paying 'em to do it to get the opium."

Hoppin' John reached down to pick up a large crab crawling over the walk and tossed it into a nearby can. "Going to have gumbo tonight. . . . I ain't saying the people here is saints. There's some mighty bad ones. But like Chang says most of 'ems mighty nice. You heard about last year when the hurricane hit?"

"What about it?" said Arkansas Ike, still defiant.

"Well, it knocked the platform next here pretty near to pieces. After a couple of days Coast Guard tried to come out to help the people on it 'cause they were sure everything they had

to eat was gone, but they couldn't get to 'em noways because the waves was so big. Finally the waves went down and the Coast Guard come and seen it was the way they figured; the people, most of 'em fishermen, was all together in a big shed on the platform that was still standing, with the water up to their knees. They was pretty near starving to death. The Coast Guard started giving meat and things to them that wanted to stay, and got ready to take the others off when they seen a dozen big fish swimming around in the water in the shed that had got trapped there someway and couldn't get out. The fish would have fed all the people there with some left over. The Coast Guard fellows couldn't figure it. 'Why didn't you kill the fish and eat 'em?' they said to the people. 'A baby could have caught them fish with two fingers.'

"The fishermen shook their heads. 'We couldn't eat them fish,' they said. 'Them fish was fighting for their lives, same as us.' "

Below me a barracuda, streamlined like a rocket for a trip to the moon, lay motionless in the water, its glaring eyes fixed on a smaller fish swimming lazily nearby. Suddenly it shot forward, its wicked teeth shining in the sunlight. The smaller fish escaped by a miracle.

Arkansas Ike spat a contemptuous cud of tobacco at the

barracuda and went on with his gloomy questioning. "What about them stories how the Chinamen when they're short of men here go to New Orleans and shanghai people, drunks and anybody they can find, and don't let 'em go till they ain't short-handed any more, just like they done on the old sailing ships?"

"Ain't nothing to it."

"Not like I heard. I heard they've caught some of the biggest people in New Orleans that way. A Jugoslav oysterman worked on the platform for a while told me once they got a big New Orleans doctor. Was a good thing they had him, too. 'Cause a big epidemic or something broke out and they'd have all died if it hadn't been for the doctor. The Jugoslav fellow knowed it to be a fact 'cause he seen the doctor himself. He cured the Jugoslav fellow of the stomachache. What do you say about that?"

"I don't know. I ain't had the stomachache."

I went around talking to the inhabitants. Because of the immense mixture of nationalities they were even more colorful than their Cajun companions deep in the marshes. So diverse were the partners in the frequent marriages, legal and illegal, the products were jocularly known by the name of a complex distillation of seafood popular in the region, a "Gumbo Filé."

Not surprisingly, they were even more superstitious than their inland brothers. For the atmosphere everywhere was one of magic and mystery. The marshes just beyond formed an eerie world that was neither land nor water, a world of giant reeds taller than a man and green floating islands that dissolved into the sea. Overhead the great man-of-war birds flew in their stately circles, and the porpoise the fisherfolk say are really men danced and played in the sunlight. It was easy to imagine that the fleecy clouds drifting across the sky and reflected in the blue water were the sails of Lafitte's pirate ships laden with the stolen treasures of the Spanish Main. It was a land like the Sahara where the horizon seemed to enclose only a world of mirages and all life seemed to be moving in a dream.

To the simple, illiterate inhabitants the sky and water were full of signs and portents. If a man happened by accident to

step on the great Congo snake that hid out in the marshes he was certain to be afflicted with a violent attack of rheumatism. If he had sinus trouble, known to the fishermen as "sun-pains," he had only to go just before daybreak to the cabin of some old woman gifted as a healer and tell her his name and the date of his birth; as the sun came up she would make the sign of the cross on his forehead and blow the pain away.

Even the cats stalking haughtily up and down the platform, fatter than prize pigs on their endless banquets of shrimp, were regarded by the older fishermen as possessing special power.

"I tell you, my friend, this is so," said Henrique, a little old Cajun with leathery face that matched his callused feet. "Maybe you think it crazy but these cats they can tell the hurricane. Ten years ago there is a cat here named Lobito, belong to a Portuguese we call Jo. This cat Lobito, when the wind going to blow, his fur get sticky like molasses, and he not eat shrimp or nothing. Only he sit and cry, like a baby when the milk in the stomach turn to gas. And in his eyes, which are green, come many white spots, like when you sprinkle sugar, maybe. It is by a cat's eyes that you tell the weather, my friend. This time the spots in Lobito's eyes are the worst I have seen. Big like rice when my wife cook it good in Lafitte. I tell you when I see this I am very afraid. I tell the other fishermen. 'There is going to be one terrible storm,' I say. 'Tie your boat with many ropes and tie it with the anchor. Maybe it is better if you go far away from here, up the Mississippi.'

"Some of the fishermen listen to me, and look at the cat and

say, 'okay, Henrique,' and tie their ropes. Some laugh and say, 'Henrique, you one big fool,' but they tie the ropes anyway. That night the hurricane come, the worst hurricane ever Barataria. It kill plenty people all over. But here nobody. It was this cat which save them, every one."

He made an expert cigarette of the tobacco I gave him. "The cats they maybe needed not so much now, maybe. The men of the Coast Guard and the radio they watch these big storm and tell the people. But ask me, my friend, and I will tell you. Between the radio and a cat like this Lobito, I will take the cat."

I continued my tour of inspection.

"I been on the platform thirty-two years come February and I sure seen some funny people," said a gnarled Mississippian sitting in front of his cabin repairing a dilapidated radio. "Couple of 'em was just plain crazy, I guess. One fellow they called the Duke, said he owned a big castle in London, and'd get awful mad if you didn't bow to him when he passed. And another fellow they called Cock-o-Doodle went strutting around everywhere cackling to himself; if you asked him a question he answered you by crowing like a rooster."

"Some pretty funny Chinamen, too," said another gnarled figure sitting beside him mending a shrimp net. "I never seen him but they said there was a big fat Chinaman wearing a kind of green nightgown wouldn't take a step if he didn't have half a dozen big Chinamen walking right behind him carrying hatchets. And another Chinaman that everywhere he went first thing he done some magic tricks, like turning your hat into a pigeon or making a little snake come out of a fountain pen. And every other day, seemed like, he was setting off shooting crackers."

"I never seen the Chinaman," said the old man with the radio. "But I seen a Italian here once with a monkey they said he'd trained to pick pockets. The monkey wouldn't touch anything except money, they said. If the money was counterfeit, he'd scratch the fellow had it to pieces."

"All monkeys can tell the difference between good and counterfeit money," said Arkansas Ike. "Better than a bank."

We passed a little cabin where a woman surrounded by half a dozen children of various ages was washing her family's clothes. "I mighty like it here on the platform," she said in the accents I knew so well of the Kentucky-Tennessee mountains. "Coal mine give out five years ago back home and my husband come here and we been ever since. Them Chinamen treats you mighty good and the people here sure is friendly."

She tugged at her youngest, so small he was barely able to stand, in imminent danger of toppling into the water. "Ain't no place to bring up a baby though. Got all I can do to keep him from falling over every minute. When I have to go to another part

of the platform I tie a bell on him like a cow. As long as I hear it ringing I know he's all right. When it stops I come a-running."

We passed the "Chinese graveyard," a curious stonelike pile so common in the region, where the waves had swept up oyster shells and formed a shallow island. Here the veteran platform-dwellers were laid to rest, unwilling to be buried out of sight of their strange wooden home.

"I tell you, my friend, after you live on the platform you not want go nowhere else," said the wrinkled Henrique, whom we came on again, chatting with a slight figure, almost as dried up as himself, who was watching a trio of pelicans flying toward the marshes. "When shrimp good you stay on platform. When shrimp bad you go in marshes trap muskrat. When you platform man you not have no trouble nowhere. Even with Indian people. Been plenty Indian people work on platforms. Plenty people say they French or Spanish when they really Indian. I tell you sure, my friend, how to find out if a man have this Indian blood. Make him to write something on a piece of paper. If he is even one small part Indian, somewhere in the writing he will put a little arrow. Indian people cannot write without putting in an arrow."

The slight figure who had been watching the pelicans introduced himself. He was Captain Frank, a self-educated naturalist who lived a life of incredible isolation beside a lonely stretch of marshes known as Devil's Island and came to the platform occasionally for supplies.

"It's no wonder the men keep coming back to the platforms," he told me. "It's a beautiful place with the clouds and the sea and the marshes, a poetic place. And these fishermen, though most of them can't write their own names, have a lot of poetry in their souls. Physically they're well off, too. The Chinese couldn't treat them more fairly. They never let any of their people go hungry. The fisherman knows he always has a roof over his head and food in his stomach so he never has to worry about money. On shore it's always money, money, money. Here nobody thinks about money."

His eyes followed a man-of-war bird circling majestically overhead. "It's like this about money. It's what an old Indian I met here told me. God made paper money and it blows away. God made silver money and it rolls away. If God had wanted you to keep money He'd have made it square like dice so it would stay where you put it."

I went to Chang's combination office and store filled with tobacco, canned goods, fishing tackle, and the usual articles required by men who live by the sea and the river. He arose from the rainbow-colored abacus with which he had been figuring his accounts and shook my hand.

I went outside and walked back with Arkansas Ike toward his boat. He gave me a furtive look and spoke quietly. "Better count your money," he said. "Them Chinamen is better than monkeys for picking your pocket. While they're shaking hands they can steal every cent you got."

CHAPTER

MUSIC
ON THE
MISSISSIPPI

Over the dark water the song drifted poignantly:

> *Roustabout ain't got no home.*
> *Makes his living from his shoulder bone.*
> *Break a line, borrow another.*
> *Black man die, hire his brother.*

The song had waked me as I lay in my bunk on the *Tennessee Belle*. I looked at my watch. It was a quarter after three in the morning. The roustabouts had finished unloading some lumber at a levee I could see starkly silhouetted by the glaring rays of the *Belle*'s searchlight. Now assured of a rest before the next landing, as they did so often in their leisure moments, they were singing a blues.

Mournfully the song continued:

Captain, I ain't comin' up here no mo',
Cause the hill's too high and the water's too low.

A new voice, a deep, rich bass worthy of a place in an opera, took over:

This ain't nothing but a monkey boat.
Don't do nothing but load and tote.

The song changed. A voice began to chant in a quavering tremolo:

What did the buzzard say to the crow?
My bail is up and I'm bound to go.

I fell asleep again as the boat started up the river. The sound of the turning paddlewheels and the soft voices of the singers were like a soothing lullaby.

I had listened to these roustabout songs often as I traveled the river. Many were work songs, to lighten their labors as they pulled at a rope or trundled wheelbarrows loaded with coal to feed the roaring fireboxes under the boilers. Many were blues, like those I had just been hearing. The blues began, the old roustabouts told me, when the outlaw women that followed the levee camps sat on the riverbank and played their mandolins and guitars, while their men who worked on the steamboats carried their heavy loads up and down the gangplank. Often the songs were about the beautiful yellow-skinned girls the roustabouts had left in New Orleans, who when their river lovers were away had quickly forgotten their promises to be faithful.

When I arose in the morning we were tied up at the Vicksburg wharfboat. I looked out and saw Piece O' Man rolling a bale of cotton. As he labored I could hear him singing a song about one of the women who had been false to her man, a buxom charmer who lived up the river near Cairo:

Where did you get them pretty little shoes?
And them clothes you wear so fine?

159

> *I got the shoes from a railroad man.*
> *And the clothes from a man in a mine.*

I never did hear the end of the story. Though maybe I did without realizing when a little while later Piece O' Man began singing:

> *Buy me a pistol.*
> *Shoot from town to town.*
> *Going to shoot you, baby.*
> *Jar your grandma down.*

All morning the roustabouts rolled the mountain of cotton on the wharfboat aboard, their half-naked sweating bodies shining like black glass. As they toiled they chanted in rhythm:

> *Vicksburg was a hilly town*
> *Till the Yankees come*
> *And cut her down.*

I left the boat and went off for a visit to the office of the US Engineers. Soon I was seated in a small boat speeding up the river. A levee camp came in sight where hundreds of black men were building a great earthen dike to protect the nearby town and the neighboring plantations from the angry river when it sought to sweep across the luxuriant countryside. Here and there men were cutting down trees to clear a space where the great dirt wall would be erected; elsewhere iron scoops were bringing dirt to make the wall higher. In one area the levee was finished; scores of black men in a long line were pulling a gigantic mat a thousand feet long and laying it over the newly piled earth so it would not be washed away by the swirling water.

In unison they chanted:

> *Shake Mattie,*
> *Lawd, Lawd.*
> *Quake Mattie,*
> *Lawd, Lawd.*

Step it, fetch it,
Lawd, Lawd.
Shake it, break it,
Lawd, Lawd.

Another group was tightening a thick steel cable linking a barge to a towboat. In chorus they sang, with the staccato rhythm of an African drum:

Bob Brown
Uptown
Got a dollar
Shore down
He win
All de money
De sucker
Put down

We left the boat in which we had come and drove back toward Vicksburg. Everywhere in the fields along the roadside black men and women were working under the scorching sun, picking cotton. Now and then we passed a mule drowsily pulling a cart loaded with firewood; the old black man sitting behind was sound asleep holding the reins.

We stopped at a little roadside café for a cooling drink. On the railroad track nearby some black men were driving spikes into newly laid ties. They were singing the innumerable verses of *John Henry*. Each blow of the sledgehammer punctuated the melody, like the crashing cymbals of a symphony orchestra:

John Henry went up to Big Stone Gap
He thought he was out of the way—Bam!
Along come a sheriff's man
Says Johnny won't you come my way—Bam!
I been to the East and I been to the West
I been this wide world round—Bam!
I been to the river and I been baptized
Take me to the hanging ground—Bam!

161

The tune and the words changed abruptly, though there was no change in the hypnotic rhythm:

> *This old hammer killed my pardner*
> *Ain't a-going to kill me—Bam!*

We drove on to a secluded cove where the shantyboats of some old friends were moored under the shade of some moss-covered live oaks. A revivalist had been in the area and the shanty-boaters in this particular colony, noted for their churchgoing, were having Holiness services at the shantyboat of a wrinkled, bright-eyed old woman known as Aunt Jessie. The neatly kept dwelling was packed with overalled men and sunbonneted women. Fervently Aunt Jessie was leading them in *Clean Train:*

> *This train's a clean train,*
> *Come on and ride.*
> *This train's the Lord's train,*
> *Come on and hide.*
> *Ain't no tobacco smokers*
> *Or ain't no gamblers,*
> *Ain't no drunkards*
> *Or midnight ramblers.*
> *This train's the Lord's train,*
> *Come on inside.*

They followed with another rivival tune:

Dancer came to the mourner's bench
Dancer she began to flench.
I asked that dancer the reason why
Other church folks dance as well as I.
That's what's the matter with the church today.

The service ended with a chant probably inspired by the Revelation of Saint John:

The Beast rolls up in the sea
The Beast rolls up in the sea
Seven heads and seven hands
And the Beast rolls up in the sea.

Nearby was the shanty of an old man known as Coal Dust Johnny who had once been a miner in the West Virginia Mountains. Now he was the accepted musician of the area, singing and playing on his guitar for celebrations at the little farms in the neighborhood. I strolled on over.

Coal Dust Johnny, whose skin seemed still to have a slightly blackish tinge from his days in the mine which endless washings could not erase, greeted me warmly.

"You ain't been around for a while," he said. "I got a new song for you. *Doodle Cap.*"

He began to sing with enthusiasm, then repeated over and over.

Old man, old man,
What makes your hair so red?
Jaybird stole my Doodle Cap
And the sun done burnt my head.

"What does it mean?" I asked.

The gray eyes in the dusty face twinkled. "Don't know. Jest Doodle Cap."

He began to sing some ballads now, starting with the *Prison-*

er's Song, whose verses, like *John Henry,* varied with each singer who added some of his own. Dolefully the strings of his guitar twanged out the melody:

> *The judge said stand up boy and dry up your tears*
> *You're sentenced to Nashville for twenty-one years.*
> *So kiss me good-by, Babe,*
> *And say you'll be mine*
> *For twenty-one years, Babe, is a mighty long time.*
> *Oh, go beg the governor on your sweet soul*
> *If you can't get a pardon try and get a parole.*

The guitar and the voice drifted easily into *Trouble on My Mind:*

> *Standing on the platform*
> *Waiting for the train*
> *I'm going down to New Orleans*
> *To wear the ball and chain.*

He continued to play, the ballads generally telling the mournful history of a misguided youth who had killed his love and was now awaiting the hangman in some bleak Southern jail, or a gory tale like that of the two dental students who had murdered the luckless Pearl Bryan and buried her head far away.

He ended with *Drunkard's Daughter:*

> *I'm alone, I'm alone,*
> *My friends have all fled*
> *My father's a drunkard,*
> *My mother is dead.*
> *I'm a lone little child,*
> *I wander and weep*
> *For the voice of my mother*
> *To sing me to sleep.*

"I ain't seen a man yet won't be pretty near crying when I play them little-girl songs like *Drunkard,*" said Coal Dust. "It'll git 'em every time."

I returned to the colony two weeks later when the *Belle* had landed at Vicksburg again, and walking over to Aunt Jessie's shanty sensed at once that something was wrong. A strange chanting was drifting out from the open doors and windows, a chanting almost Oriental in its eerie melancholy. I quickly learned the reason as I walked aboard the little craft, again crowded with people. But Aunt Jessie was no longer leading them with her eager, quavering voice; instead she was lying in her neat bed, desperately ill with fever. Surrounding the bed were her shanty-boat neighbors, singing a song I had never heard before and never heard afterward, *O Death*. The chant was a dramatic plea to Death to stay away from the shantyboat and keep Aunt Jessie from dying:

> *"What is this that I can see*
> *With icy hands taking hold of me?"*
> *"I am Death and none can't tell*
> *I open doors to Heaven and Hell.*
> *I'll fix your feet so you can't walk*
> *I'll lock your jaws so you can't talk.*
> *I'll close your eyes so you can't see*
> *This very hour come and go with me."*

And then the strange chorus, repeated over and over:

> *"O Death! O Death! O Death!*
> *Please spare me over till another year."*

To my delight the ritual seemed highly effective. When I returned a week later Aunt Jessie was on her back porch with a hook and line, catching a catfish for her supper.

I continued my travels on the *Belle,* stopping to explore every little town, going ashore at every landing. Everywhere I went there was music.

I stepped off the gangplank at New Orleans one afternoon to see a crowd of roustabouts and a few white passersby gathered in a corner of the docks. Walking forward to investigate I discovered they were gathered about an old black man with a fringe of white beard framing a face wrinkled like an ancient Egyptian scroll. Fixed to a guitar he was holding was a battered harmonica; attached to his right foot was a padded stick that beat a shabby bass drum; on his left foot was a device that caused cymbals to clash deafeningly. On all four instruments, as a one-man band, he was playing *Dixie*.

As I watched, he put away all the instruments except the harmonica, and placing this in his mouth, began playing *Chattanooga Express*. At the same time he executed a curious shuffling dance, imitating a fireman on a locomotive shoveling coal, then shifted his feet, moving ever faster and faster to imitate the movement of the wheels, while the music of the harmonica imitated the frantic chugging of the engine. Soon after, he began the Buzzard Dance, flapping his arms like the gloomy bird's wings as he circled an imaginary object on the dark floor, like a buzzard investigating a possible dead body.

"That's old Jugging Joe," explained Piece O' Man who was standing near me. "He can dance a hundred and one cutting steps."

The chugging train gave way to a military march; the old man shouldered arms with an imaginary rifle and then rushed forward in a fierce bayonet charge. "Now he's doing a soldier in the Spanish War," said Piece O' Man. "Now he's doing a policeman shooting at a robber and the robber's gitting away to the swamps. When he dances the robber a-running you can hear him clear over to Canal Street."

Even the dogs on the river were musical. I came off the *Belle* at Baton Rouge not long after to get a haircut, and was sitting in a barbershop near the wharf, when a cadaverous individual carrying a guitar entered, followed by a dog whose ancestry was so mixed not even the most distinguished members of the College of Heraldry could ever trace his bizarre origins. His head was almost big enough for that of a St. Bernard; his small body was like that of a Scotch terrier; his short pudgy legs were almost those of a dachshund. His eyes were half closed; his ambition seemed to be to sleep for the rest of his life.

The cadaverous man and his companion were obviously well known to the barber. He put down his scissors a moment and turned to the dog, whose eyes were fixed drowsily on the floor. "You going to play us some music today, Tobe?"

The dog's half-shut eyes opened a fraction of an inch farther. He raised his head a trifle and gave a single sleepy bark.

"He says okay," the barber told me.

The cadaverous man took a seat on a vacant chair and placed the guitar on his lap.

"Play *Shimbo Nanny*," he told the dog.

At the words the dog laboriously stood up on his hind legs, and resting one front paw on a knee of the cadaverous man, brushed the other paw across the strings of the guitar. A weird discord resulted, like the tuning up of an orchestra composed of the inmates of an asylum. He continued to strike the strings like a drowsy automaton, while the cadaverous man awkwardly fingered the scarred frets above.

"He can play any tune there is," said the cadaverous man as the music ended and the dog relapsed into his earlier state of half-consciousness. "He's special good at them high-class songs like *Adeline*. . . . You ain't got a spare dime, have you, Mister? Seems like people don't like music way they used to."

I left the *Belle* and began wandering through the countryside.
I went into the moss-fringed bayous of the Evangeline country.
Here many of the songs were old French tunes, sometimes changed
almost beyond recognition by distance and time. Occasionally,
however, I would come upon a cabin where a lonely Anglo-Saxon
trapper, over cups of fragrant coffee, would sing me a ballad in
English, like *Pontchartrain:*

> *Early, early one evening*
> *In the merry month of May*
> *Through swamps and alligators*
> *I made my weary way.*
> *O'er railroad ties and crossings*
> *To some fair land I came*
> *It was there I met the Creole girl*
> *On the banks of the Pontchartrain.*

I began moving up the tributaries, the Missouri and the
Arkansas, the Black and the Ouchita. Everywhere it was the same;
music, simple though it might be, was an integral part of the life
of the people.

I went up the Ohio and into the Cumberland, up the rocky
forks and creeks that led back into the remote mountains. I spent
many days in the village jails, listening to the songs of the unshaven inmates as they played their shabby guitars or harmonicas.
Songs like:

> *You can't never believe*
> *What a young man tells you*
> *Unless he's on the gallows*
> *And wishing he was down.*

Always I carried a mandolin; when I stopped in a log cabin
to eat or sleep with a little encouragement I would tinkle out *Old
Black Joe* or *Swanee River*. The mandolin was my peace pipe and
my protection if any of my hosts happened to be making moonshine liquor. Revenue officers didn't play musical instruments.

Every day I would come upon a new song, sometimes tragic, sometimes gay, sometimes propounding a riddle. Often the verses would be filled with melancholy philosophy, like *Big Bee:*

> *The big bee makes the honey*
> *The little bee makes the comb*
> *The poor man fights the battle*
> *The rich man stays at home.*
> *Sparrow on the mountain*
> *A sparrow trying to crow*
> *A dead man trying to shave himself*
> *And a blind man trying to sew.*

Or it might be only a few lines that revealed a whole mountain drama:

> *Mother, dear mother, I love you so well*
> *But the love I have for the gambler man*
> *No woman's tongue can tell.*

I had been in the Cumberlands for several weeks, riding horseback through the secluded hollows, when I came on a little town where I was given overwhelming evidence of the power of music, a power unknown in the cities which boast their great concert halls and magnificent orchestras. I had remained in the settlement for several days, riding out into the country each morning to listen to some wrinkled singer or tobacco-chewing old fiddler, when the wide-sombreroed sheriff of the area came up to me. "Brother, there's a fellow over in the jail for moonshining we call Soupy Doc's heard you was here gitting old songs and things. He says he'd like you to come over to the jail and listen to him sing."

I didn't respond to the invitation at once. I had already arranged a number of meetings, and since I learned that Soupy Doc was going to be in jail for some time to come, I didn't feel there was any need to hurry. But before another day passed Soupy Doc had sent two more leading officials of the town to urge me to pay him a visit. Finally the local Judge himself called at the tiny ram-shackle hotel where I was stopping.

"Soupy Doc wants you to come mighty bad, brother," the Judge told me. "He says he's got some mighty fine songs for you."

I couldn't any longer resist a request coming through such important judicial channels and hurried over to the jail. Soupy Doc was eagerly awaiting my appearance, a gaunt, drowsy-eyed individual who reminded me of the dog that had played the guitar in the barbershop at Baton Rouge. While the other pris-oners gathered round he took a dilapidated guitar made of a cigar box from a shelf and tuned the strings.

"You ever heard *Fox Race?*" he demanded.

I shook my head.

"I knowed you hadn't. If you listen right you can hear the dogs barking."

He began to play expertly, his deft, quick-moving fingers belying his sleepy face, the strings sometimes, as he had said, giv-ing the effect of the baying of the hounds.

He ended and turned to me again. "You ever heard *Napo-leon's Retreat?*"

I shook my head again.

"Knowed you hadn't. If you listen right you can hear them Russian cannons shooting."

For most of the afternoon he played, his repertoire ranging from interpretative pieces like those he had just rendered to the usual dismal mountain tales of false love and murder.

Several days later Circuit Court opened, an event accom-panied each session by an old fiddlers' contest. My praise of Soupy Doc was so enthusiastic he was permitted to leave jail and take part in the competition. Unanimously the judges awarded him first prize. Next day, though his sentence still had a considerable time to run I saw him walking about the town, wearing the tight white-duck suit he had borrowed for the contest. The authorities had properly decided that the community's leading musical talent could not be confined by prison bars and had given Soupy Doc his liberty.

The hills about the little town were crowded with musicians of all varieties. A few days later I was at a crossroads store and chanced to come on Fiddling Jack, the saber-mustached musical master of his valley.

The mountaineers sitting around the empty stove serving as a cuspidor looked on in admiration as the old man picked up the cracked violin lying on the counter.

"Jack's a wonderful fiddler," said a lanky farmer whose overalls were flecked with the feed he had been giving his horse.

"Can't beat Jack for fiddling," said the farmer next him, patting with his foot the lean dog stretched out under his chair. "Fellow from Chicago was here a while ago and heard him and said wasn't nobody in Chicago or New York or any place could get anywhere near him."

Fiddling Jack set the violin against his shoulder and turned toward me. "What'll I play you, brother?"

"I'll be happy to hear anything you like."

"I'll play you *Fire on the Mountain*."

"That's a pretty piece, *Fire on the Mountain*," said the farmer with the flecked overalls.

"*Fire on the Mountain*'s a mighty pretty piece," said the farmer with the dog.

171

Fiddling Jack began to ply the bow valiantly. "Ee-ya-ya-ya. Ee-ya-ya-ya," whined the strings in toneless monotony.

He ended. The farmers sitting about the stove nodded approval.

"That's sure a pretty piece, *Fire on the Mountain*," said the farmer with the overalls.

"It's as fine a piece as there is," said the farmer with the dog. "And Jack's sure a wonderful fiddler."

Fiddling Jack turned to me again. "What'll I play you now, brother?"

"Play anything you like, Jack."

"I'll play you *Billy in the Low Ground*."

"That's a mighty pretty piece, *Billy in the Low Ground*," said the overalled farmer.

"It's a beautiful piece, *Billy in the Low Ground*," said the farmer with the dog.

Again Fiddling Jack began to ply the bow; again the violin began to whine tonelessly. "Ee-ya-ya-ya. Ee-ya-ya-ya."

As far as my ears could distinguish the old man was still playing *Fire on the Mountain*.

"What'll I play you now, brother?" he asked when the solo was finished.

"Whatever you feel like, Jack."

"I'll play you *Old Joe Clark*."

"That's a beautiful piece, *Old Joe Clark*," said the farmer with the dog.

A third and a fourth and a twentieth time, for almost two hours the fiddle droned out the same dreary sounds, "Ee-ya-ya-ya. Ee-ya-ya-ya." Everything was *Fire on the Mountain*. I could not detect the difference of a single note.

The old man's eyes settled on the mandolin I was carrying. "Brother, I see you got a guitar there," he declared. "Brother, how about you and me playing a duet?"

I agreed at once. The only piece we both knew was *Kentucky Home*, and I began to strum the melody. I trilled away with

enthusiasm for a moment and then I noticed something was terribly wrong. I stopped my playing and listened. The fiddle was scraping out "Ee-ya-ya-ya. Ee-ya-ya-ya." It was *Fire on the Mountain.*

I play duets no more.

I returned to the river and the *Tennessee Belle.* The boat stopped alongside the wharf at Natchez Under the Hill to take on some cattle; I listened as a giant black man known as Crazy Tom sang the sorrowful verses of *Eagle Nest:*

> *Eagle build his nest so high*
> *Cannot hear his young ones cry.*
> > *Dark and cloudy.*
> *He can hardly see the day.*
> *Please, O Lord, then show me the way.*
> > *Dark and cloudy.*
> *I'm trying to go where my young ones is*
> *And my home is hard to find.*

The musicians I knew up the Cumberland and on the shantyboats have long since put away their fiddles and guitars, and Crazy Tom no longer sings on the wharf at Natchez Under the Hill. The *Tennessee Belle* lies at the bottom of the river and the chanting of her roustabouts has ended. Yet I hope that somewhere on a shantyboat in a moss-covered cove or in a cabin up a pine-bordered mountain stream someone like Coal Dust Johnny or Soupy Doc is playing *Letters Have No Arms* or *I Have No Mother Now*. I hope that somewhere a white-haired roustabout on his peaceful little farm looks out at the Mississippi winding to the horizon and sings as he sang when he was sailing its muddy waters:

> *River is so deep and wide,*
> *Can't call my baby from the other side.*

PART

THE WAY
IT
IS TODAY

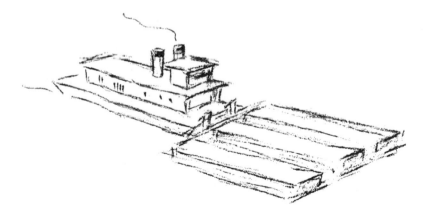

CHAPTER

A VOYAGE
OF
ROSES

"It ain't the same Mississippi you knew noways," said Long Jack, the lean Arkansas deckhand who had come up to the dark pilot house to make some fresh coffee for us on the hot plate in a corner. "Ain't no more like she used to be than a old Ozark mule's like a ten-thousand-dollar automobile."

The genial young pilot, Captain Paul Hight, swept the great searchlight across the row after row of barges we were pushing that stretched before him almost a quarter of a mile. He swung the levers controlling the rudders and brought the lead barge in line with the channel light flashing in the distance. "Long Jack's said it right," he declared. "Forty years ago all you had in a pilot house was a big steering wheel broke your back to turn and a speaking tube to cuss out the engineer. Now we've got as many gadgets as the astronauts going to the moon."

He clicked on the electric light an instant so that I could see the dazzling array of navigation instruments surrounding us everywhere: the steering levers and the other levers that controlled the engines, the radar that showed every faintest obstruction on the river a mile ahead, the automatic pilot, the fathometer that indicated the depth of the water over which we were traveling.

A wizened, snowy-haired old man sitting on a stool near the pilot shifted uneasily. "One of them old ladies used to drive them electric automobiles could run a towboat nowadays," he said tartly.

The light went out.

We were in the pilot house of the towboat *American Beauty* of the Rose Barge Line of St. Louis, bound downriver to New Orleans. Lashed to our prow, locked into a solid mass by thick steel cables and heavy ratchets, were forty-two enormous barges, the equivalent of many freight trains, loaded to capacity with 42,000 tons of wheat and corn and soy beans from the rich farms of Missouri and Iowa and Illinois.

I looked out a pilot-house window. Behind us we could see a shimmering glow of light in the sky, like Aurora Borealis, that marked some industrial town in the area of St. Louis which we had left a few hours before. Ahead of us stretched the river, black, mysterious.

A storm had been threatening since our departure. Now a

streak of lightning with great fiery branches like a golden tree circled halfway around the horizon, followed by a rumble of thunder.

"Here she comes," said Captain Paul. A torrent of rain beat against the pilot-house windows, forming an opaque watery curtain that for a moment blotted out all sight of the river. The windshield-wiper began to swish back and forth noisily.

A new blinding flash cleft the sky and another and another. Captain Paul glanced at the radar circling eerily beside him, and kept the boat moving steadily on its way.

"It's a new river," repeated Long Jack. "Old times in a storm like this a steamboat'd run for the bank and tuck her nose in the trees like a rabbit running from a weasel."

I remembered how my favorite steamboat, the *Tennessee Belle*, with her high wooden superstructure that turned her into a gigantic sail, had always dashed to the woods at the first threat of a storm, lest the wind blow her over. These new, solidly built Diesel towboats continued on their way unmindful of stormy weather; they could resist anything but a hurricane. The engines of the *American Beauty* developed 5000 horsepower; the *Tennessee Belle* had 250.

The storm ended as quickly as it had begun, to be succeeded by a heavy mist that swirled about us like the robes of drifting ghosts.

Paul slackened speed and watched the radar intently again.

The snowy-haired man, a retired old-time steamboat mate known as Captain Clem, like myself was a guest of the line, in the long-honored tradition of river hospitality. He lit a pungent stogie. "Didn't need no radar for fog in the old days. Old times you'd blow the whistle and listen for the echo and that way you could tell how far you were from the land. Never seen it done myself but I heard of pilots blowing a whistle to get the frogs on the bank to croaking back."

The fog lifted. A towboat loomed up in the darkness and Captain Paul blew two blasts of our whistle, indicating that we would pass the other boat on our right; one blast would have meant passing on our left. The choice of whistles was at the discretion of Captain Paul. The swift current and the speed of a vessel coming downstream made it much more difficult to control than a boat making its way slowly up the river. The downstream boat always had the right-of-way.

At the same instant the oncoming boat whistled in answer two flashes of light appeared above its pilot house.

"That's something else new on the river, the whistle light," said Captain Paul. "Riverman that invented it said some captains might be deaf and some captains might be blind, but the whistle light'd take care of 'em 'cause he didn't know any pilot that was deaf and blind both."

"Pilot in the old days wouldn't stop till he was halfway in his coffin," grunted Captain Clem. "Not like these pilots today. I knew a pilot could hardly see, but he had the mate standing right by him to tell him if the buoy they were passing was black or red, so he'd know which side he ought to go."

The boat chugged onward.

Captain Paul picked up the radio telephone beside him. *"American Beauty.* Calling all traffic northbound around Devil's Island. Over."

There was a moment's pause; then a metallic Southern voice came over the loudspeaker. *"Carrie C.* back to the *American Beauty.* What channel do you want, Captain?"

"I'll take Eleven, Captain. I'll take Channel Eleven."

The channel of which they were speaking was not one in the river but a channel of the radio. Immediately after establishing contact pilots switched to a secondary frequency so as to leave the main channel always open for emergencies.

Captain Paul adjusted the radio. *"American Beauty* to the *Carrie C.* back. Where are you, Captain? Where are you? Over."

'I'm at Cape Rock, Captain. I'm at Cape Rock. How many whistles you want, Captain?"

"I'll take two whistles, Captain. I'll take two whistles. Thank you, Captain."

This was also something new on the river, these radio conversations. In the old days if a boat was lucky enough to have a radio ninety percent of the time it didn't work. Now, I quickly learned, it was a vital part of the river's navigation. It enabled a pilot to plan the position he would take in the river at the other boat's approach and so avoid an accident.

Suddenly there was a terrific rumble beneath us that made the hull tremble from bow to stern.

"Just a wheel inspector," said Captain Paul. "Drifting log caught in a propeller tunnel."

He sent the engines into reverse. The great propellers spun deafeningly and cast out the offender as a sea animal spews out some too prickly fish.

By the glare of the searchlight Long Jack watched the huge log drift away. "Old-time days she'd have knocked a hole in a steamboat quicker than a Arkansas preacher can pick out a counterfeit nickel."

I left the pilot house and went below to the galley for a snack. Wayne, the stocky mate, and Roy, a baby-faced deckhand, were sitting at a table drinking coffee.

We talked of the new disease on the river known as Channel Fever, like the Cabin Fever of the Arctic that develops in the endless winter night. Here the fever, an acute homesickness, resulted because the crews of the boats, mostly married men, were away from their wives and children for thirty-one days at a time and often longer. Moreover, they were unable to leave the boat for a moment as the vessel, except when it went into dry dock for repairs, never touched the shore; a far cry from the days when a packetboat stopped wherever a farmer on the bank waved his battered hat or an old black woman stood waiting with two pigtailed children and a broken stove.

Long Jack, come down from the pilot house, joined in the conversation. "Gets so bad only way you can tell the day of the week is by what the cook gives you to eat. Wednesday and Sunday you have chicken. Friday you have fish. Saturday you have steak. The rest of the week you dont' know if it's Monday, Tuesday, or Thursday."

We helped ourselves to a luscious strawberry pie a gourmet cook might have envied. "Eats ain't like they used to be," said the baby-faced Roy. "Old days way I heard you didn't get nothing but rice and beans. Cooking on the boats now's like eating in them fancy restaurants in New Orleans."

Wayne brought a new pot of coffee to the table. "Louis Reitz in St. Louis was telling me he worked on a old-time boat where all the cook had was a big iron pot on the stove and a spoon hanging from the ceiling. He'd ask you what you wanted, soup or stew. If you said soup he dipped the spoon in the top of the pot. If you said stew he dug down to the bottom."

"You can get a boat as bad as that nowadays if the captain and the cook's both crazy about playing poker," put in Long Jack. "They sit up all night playing and all the crew gets is cold cuts."

Wayne filled my cup from the steaming pot. "A towboat runs half on Diesel oil and half on coffee," he said.

I went to bed soon after.

I awoke early in the morning and went down to the galley again. Captain Paul and Long Jack and Bill, the chief engineer, just emerged from their comfortable, air-conditioned cabins, were having breakfast. Marie, the dark-haired, much-traveled cook, and Margie, the vivacious maid, were serving hot cakes and sausages and ham and eggs and hot biscuits and corn bread. In the old days a woman as cook or maid on a boat was a rarity; now it was a common practice, though the women were generally beyond the age where they might cause amorous complications.

"Good thing to have women on a boat," said Bill, the engineer. "Makes you shave and be polite. Women cooks are mostly widows. Most men cooks are winos."

I went up to the pilot house. We were at Cairo, almost an island in the flatlands of that southernmost section of Illinois known as Little Egypt, where the Ohio empties into the Mississippi. Several tugs were moving about us rearranging our tow. It was a complicated affair, shifting these barges, much like the shunting of freight cars in a railroad yard. While the towboat,

with her engines at slow speed, held the main body of the tow stationary near the shore, the tugs moved busily about her, now and then pulling out a barge and tying it up to the bank, or bringing another barge out from the darkness and adding it to the tow. It was a process requiring several hours, but a far different method from that in the old days when all the work was done by the towboat, sometimes requiring an entire day. Time was costly on these great new vessels like the *American Beauty;* every hour when the boats were not moving their cargoes on to their destinations meant a loss of hundreds of dollars.

The watch had changed and another pilot was at the control levers now, the commander of the vessel, Captain Jim Bell, a quiet man who spoke with long pauses between each sentence.

The tow, now forty-five barges, was finished soon after breakfast. We started down the river once more. The Mississippi was wider, swelled with the waters of the Ohio. We were moving close to the shore, lined with willows stretching to the horizon. Captain Jim was watching the clocklike face of the fathometer; the electronic indicator marking the depth of the water under the foremost barges was flickering giddily.

He spoke to the tall second mate standing near him. "Get one of the boys out to the head of the tow to fix that contact, Larry. The fathometer's gone haywire again."

The other hurried off.

"Lot better when you just had a roustabout throwing a lead line and singing out the soundings," mumbled Captain Clem. "Lot prettier, too."

A tow of steel coming down from Pittsburgh appeared behind us, followed by a giant tow of coal from the mountains of West Virginia. Ahead of us four other tows were visible—including ourselves a total of seven huge tows within two miles. In the Twenties and Thirties if two or three boats passed in twenty-four hours it was accounted a busy day. The river trade, because of its low cost, since the war had been increasing at a phenomenal rate. Towboat- and barge-builders were two years behind in their orders. On the Inland Waterways there were 4250 towboats and tugs; most of these were on the Mississippi and its tributaries and connections. It was estimated that a tenth of the country's commerce now moved along these watery routes that had been almost deserted since the turn of the century.

"River's getting as crowded as Canal Street in New Orleans in Mardi Gras," said Captain Jim.

A red buoy showed ahead marking the channel. Captain Jim swung the tow to keep well inside.

"Didn't have the buoys put out by the Coast Guard to show you how to go in my time," grunted Captain Clem. "You had to know every snag and every sand bar and every tree on the river. Had to know 'em at night, too. Pilots' eyes them days was better than a cat."

The current was faster now. We were speeding down the river at twelve miles an hour.

I had lunch and with Captain Clem returned to the pilot house.

The old man looked out at the brown water swirling over some stone dikes stretching far out in the stream to deflect the current. "They think they've got this river tamed," he said to Captain Paul who was once more at the controls. "But they ain't. She's like a tiger, just laying low."

Captain Paul swept the tow past the dikes and picked up the radio telephone. *"American Beauty.* Calling all traffic northbound in New Madrid Bend. Over."

Instantly there came back the answer. *"Cherokee* to the *American Beauty.* What channel, Captain? What channel?"

"I'll take Channel Eight, Captain. I'll take Eight." He flicked the lever of the radio. *"American Beauty* back. Where are you, Captain? Where are you? Over."

"I'm in the Bend at Morrison Towhead Foot Light, Captain. At Morrison Towhead Foot Light. How many whistles you want, Captain?"

"I'll take one whistle, Captain. I'll take one whistle. Over."

"Okay, okay. I'll lay here near the Light till you pass, Captain. Don't want to give you any trouble. I'll lay here near the Light. Who's this? Paul?"

"That's right. That's right. Who's this?"

"It's Marty, Paul. It's Marty. How's the coon-hunting?"

"Not doing much coon-hunting these days, Marty."

"Well, if you do I'll tell you the best way, Paul. Drill a hole in a block of wood and put a shiny nickel at the bottom. The coon'll put in his paw to get it. Can pull the paw out any time he wants to but he won't. He's worse than a Scotchman. Rather be caught than give up the nickel."

His raucous laughter made the loudspeaker quiver.

Paul winked at me as he covered the mouthpiece with his hand. "Used to work with Marty. He'll talk for an hour on the radio if you let him." He put his mouth to the phone again. "Guess I better let you go now, Marty. Guess I better let you go."

"Guess you better, Paul. I guess you better. I got to look after the potatoes I'm growing on my barges in the dirt come from them steel towns up the Ohio. Did you hear about that steel barge pretty near went over the dam at Lock—"

"I'll let you go now, Marty," said Paul quickly. "I'll let you go." With a grin he put the telephone back on the hook.

All day and into the night we sped, past River Styx Lower Light and Forked Deer Light and Gold Dust Bar Light, past New Madrid and Caruthersville and Luxora. Memphis appeared before us, blazing with light. But we did not stop. Instead a store boat, the *Contact,* came out from shore bringing our laundry and groceries.

The store boat chugged away.

The two shadowy bridges at Memphis loomed ahead.

Captain Paul grew intent. "These bridges were bad enough with a steamboat. Railroads built 'em that way to kill the river trade. Now with these big tows we've got it's like the fellow in a sideshow throws knives at his wife. One slip and you're a goner."

As expertly as a sharpshooter aims his rifle, he aimed the lead barges at the narrow space between the piers. I held my breath as the tow glided through the racing waters, with only a few feet to spare on either side.

The night and another day passed. Another store boat came out from Greenville harbor to meet us and moored alongside as we raced down the water. I hurried aboard. In a microscopic space was collected everything a riverman might desire: razors, work clothes, candy, cigarettes, but chiefly girlie books and girlie magazines.

Long Jack was standing beside me, making a quick selection. "Fellow'd get mighty educated if he could read all the books they got on a store boat."

Two more days and the skyscrapers that marked New Orleans came into sight on the horizon. I disembarked with Captain Clem and took a sister ship, the *Crimson Glory,* bound with a new tow of thirty-three barges up the river. Appropriately, all the towboats of the Rose Line were named for famous varieties of the flower.

Dawn was breaking as I went up to the pilot house where young Captain Johnson, known as Junior, was at the controls. I had learned on the *American Beauty* that on the modern Mississippi there were no longer any titles. The crews were mostly young country boys, with all the young generation's disregard for formality. Deckhands called the captain and the mates by their first names.

Great oil tankers and smaller ocean vessels known as Mini Ships were speeding past us constantly. Now and then a tug glided by, pushing some curious-shaped barges called Lash Lighters, the latest development in container freight. Arrived in New Orleans each barge would be lifted by a giant crane onto a mother ship and stowed away for a voyage across the Atlantic, then deposited again for a further adventure on some European canal.

"Don't know what they'll figure out next," said Captain Clem. "Even seen some Hippies working on some of the tugs with hair coming down to their waist. If Captain Cannon of the *Robert E. Lee* or Captain Leathers of the *Natchez* seen that they'd turn over in their graves."

Long Jack had been due his thirty-one days' leave on the *American Beauty,* but instead had come on the *Crimson Glory* to earn some extra money as a relief deckhand. With Danny, another youthful riverman, he was polishing the brightwork in the pilot house. "Hippies like the towboats account of the pay," he declared. "Ain't like the old days when you got a dollar a day."

"Now you get twenty," said Danny. "With a day off for every day you work and get paid all the time besides."

"Deckhand's always got plenty of money on him," added Long Jack. "Spends it, too. Deckhand'll take a taxi, but the captains walk." He rubbed a cloth vigorously across the fathometer. "Carry so much cash on 'em there's one town on this river—I ain't mentioning no names—that I figure's got a special radar to spot a deckhand, they arrest him so quick. They throw him in jail and the judge fines him in the morning. If he's got $400 in his pocket the fine's $395."

"Knew a deckhand went ashore with $2000," said Danny. "Come back in a week and all he had left was a pair of new shoes and they was too little for him."

We were going slowly now. Instead of our swift pace downstream we were traveling only three or four miles an hour.

The watches changed at lunchtime. The slight Junior was succeeded by Captain Gene Holder, an amiable broad-chested Kentuckian nicknamed Big Red.

"Don't have as many funny characters as in the old days," declared Big Red. "It's a young man's river and they ain't ripened yet. Knew one funny one, though, down on the Houston Canal. Used to get crazy drunk and one day came rushing out of his cabin yelling his head off. "Anybody here got a mongoose?" he hollered. "I want a mongoose quick!"

"What you want a mongoose for?" we asked him.

"My cabin's full of snakes!" he yelled. "I want a mongoose to kill 'em!"

I grew worried as a light on an instrument board beside me began flashing wildly; an electronic alarm began to wail like the siren of a police car on its way to a holdup. Jimmy, the stocky chief engineer, hurried up from below and changed a fuse.

He remained to chat a moment. "I was on a boat with a funny character once. Was in the galley having a bite when the captain came in and started eating too. I knew he was supposed to be up in the pilot house and I asked him who was steering the boat.

" 'My wife's running her,' he said, and a second later we crashed into the bank. He was a spiritualist; his wife had died three years before."

I went below with Jimmy to the engine room, deafening with the roar of the Diesel engines turning the enormous propellers. There was no resemblance to the engine rooms I had known on the old steamboats. Instead of the boilers with the sweating black firemen tossing coal and the great wooden arms that turned the paddlewheels, like the pilot house it was crowded with electronic equipment that made it appear to have been lifted bodily from a science-fiction movie.

I asked about the ancient feud between the engineers and the pilots.

Jimmy chuckled. "Pretty well ended, I guess, when the pilot began running the engines from the pilot house. But an engineer can still make plenty of trouble for a pilot he don't like—slowing down the generators so the pilot doesn't have enough power when he's in a tight spot, and the boat goes up on a sand bar or maybe smashes up a barge." He glanced at the fuel gauge a moment. "My father was an engineer in the old days. He told me that whenever there was a ring from the pilot house he'd always look out at the river to see if the pilot was right. If he didn't think so he just sort of forgot."

I went with him into the galley for supper, presided over by Fern, the bright-faced, kindly maid, and the tall, intellectual Virginia, the cook.

We sat around talking after the meal.

"Don't have pets on the boats way they used to," said George, the lanky mate, who a hundred years before might have been the sheriff in a cattle town of the West. "Crews change too often. Had a pigeon on the *Glory* for a while we called Herman. Flew on at Cairo and rode down to New Orleans. When we got back to Cairo he flew off with a lady pigeon that was there on the bank waiting for him. Guess he wanted to see the world a little before he settled down."

I returned to the pilot house. Black storm clouds were sweeping across the sky as on the voyage downward, blotting out the pale stars. A new deluge beat against the pilot-house windows. The battering rain and the howling wind joined with the eerie swishing of the window-wiper and the mournful sighing of the circling radar to form a ghostly symphony. By the glare of the great searchlight I could see George, the mate, and two of the deckhands going out on the barges to tighten the lines. The yellow life-preservers strapped to their backs glowed like phosphorus.

Heavy waves touched with foam began dancing about us. The wind increased, whistling through the pilot house with demoniac fury.

Captain Clem's gaze was fixed on the raging water. "She's like a tiger," he repeated.

The mate and the two deckhands, fighting the storm, made their way slowly across the barges back to the boat.

"Dangerous business on these barges a night like this," commented Big Red as Long Jack, streaming with water, came in from the darkness. "Too easy to fall in the river."

Long Jack shivered and shook the water from his raincoat. "Ain't as bad falling in here as in that Chicago Drainage Canal when you come to Chicago out of the Illinois River. If you fall in there they won't pull you back onto your boat you smell so bad. They just let you drown."

Day after day we continued up the river, gloomy, ominous skies alternating with periods of glorious sunlight. Baton Rouge and Natchez and Vicksburg drifted behind us.

A towboat pushing some empty gasoline barges appeared in the distance with a red flag ahead indicating danger. The channel was narrow here, hemmed in by dikes and sand bars; I could tell by the floating drift that the current was swift as a mountain rapids.

"Empty gas barges are bad as an atom bomb," said Big Red at the controls. "Gas left in 'em after they're pumped out'll blow up if you sneeze. Give 'em plenty of room." He picked up the radio telephone. *"Crimson Glory* calling the gas tow at Possum Chute Lower Light. Over."

Contact was quickly established. The other towboat was named the *Catahoula.*

"Crimson Glory to the *Catahoula* back. How many whistles you want, Captain?"

"I'll take one whistle, Captain. I'll take one whistle. Who's this? Junior?"

"Nope. It's Big Red."

"That's fine, Red. That's fine. How's them three hunting dogs you paid all that money for?"

"They're fine, Captain. Who's this? Lew?"

"That's right, Red. It's Lew all right. You been doing any fox-racing up in your country, Red?"

"I ain't much for fox-racing, Lew."

"I like it, Red. I like it. Ain't nothing better to me than to hear the dogs hollering. I got a couple of 'em that sing like Caruso, Red."

"That's fine, Lew. That's fine."

"Bad thing pretty near happened last time we was fox-racing, Red. Fellow come from up North went out with us over near Eudora and was going to shoot the fox. He didn't know fox-racing's just to hear the dogs singing. We stopped him in time. Hear about the fellow was fox-racing over at Little Rock, Red?"

"No, I haven't, Lew."

"Well, this fellow's dogs didn't come back in the morning after running all night and he had to go back to town without 'em. He'd heard if you left your coat they'd come to the coat, so he put

it down where they'd been racing. When he come back that afternoon the dogs was there sure enough. But the coat was gone."

"I better let you go now, Lew. I better let you go."

The gas barges approached with what seemed the speed of an
express train. Red swung our tow to give them a wide berth.

The gas barges swept down the river.

Another day passed. I sat for a few minutes after supper in
the crew's air-conditioned lounge where on a color television
screen the latest astronauts were walking on the moon, then went
below to the stainless-steel galley with its latest in electric ovens
and complicated blenders and every other fancy gadget that made
it the equal of the kitchen of the most ultramodern hotel.

"It's sure a new river," Long Jack said.

We started to drink the usual coffee.

Suddenly from above there sounded four quick blasts of the
whistle, the signal for an emergency. An instant later there came a
tremendous crash ahead that rocked the lumbering vessel like an
earthquake.

We rushed from the galley onto the deck. To my horror
instead of thirty-three barges lashed to the bow there were now
only three. The vague shapes of other barges were racing in all
directions about us, like huge marine animals running from a
tidal wave. Not far away I could see a shadowy towboat disappearing into the night. We dashed up to the pilot house.

Junior was at the radiophone, tense, but cool. "This is an
emergency. This is an emergency. *Crimson Glory* at mile 598 in
Scrubgrass Bend. Calling all vessels in the area. We have been hit
by another boat. Request all assistance. Request all assistance. We
are at mile 598 in Scrubgrass Bend. This is an emergency."

He picked up another telephone near him. "*Crimson Glory*
calling the mobile operator, Helena. This is an emergency. Please
get me the Coast Guard. This is an emergency."

Almost instantaneously the radio telephone was crackling
with an answering message. "*Mountain Home* to the *Crimson
Glory. Mountain Home* to the *Crimson Glory*. We are tying up
our tow and coming to your assistance."

191

Two other similar messages came quickly from two tugs nearby. In a few minutes the three vessels arrived and began corralling the straying barges, much as cowboys round up a herd of cattle after a stampede, blocking their path or swinging to one side as a barge hurtled past, like a cowboy throwing a lasso.

A hasty inspection showed that the *Crimson Glory* was undamaged. But at least one barge was sinking. One of the tugs towed it into shallow water along the shore.

The shadowy boat which had caused the accident stayed off in the distance.

Daylight came and the three vessels that had hurried to our rescue were still rounding up barges and helping the *Glory* remake the tow. The sinking barge that had borne the brunt of the shock was tied up at the bank, to await a tug that would take it to drydock in New Orleans. If the towboat that struck us had been 175 feet closer and hit the *Crimson Glory* instead of the barges we might all have been at the bottom of the river.

The atmosphere grew calmer and we learned what had happened. The other towboat was speeding downriver around Scrubgrass Bend. Suddenly the pilot saw the *Crimson Glory* dead ahead and swung his controls to veer away. But the Mississippi, asserting itself as it had done so many times in the past, decided again to take command. Despite the complex instruments in the pilot house, the perfection of all that modern marine science could devise, despite the massive engines designed to meet such crises with the strength of 5000 horses, the boat continued on its headlong way. Some hidden current seized the hull like the grip of a giant hand and left the pilot powerless. The river, not man, was still the master.

Our tow was reassembled at last. With thirty-two barges we moved slowly up the stream.

Captain Clem looked out at the murky water. "She's the same old river," he said.